ADVANCE PRAISE

"Vanstone takes us on a romp through the chaotic origin of modern roller derby; the highs and lows, the incredible people who play this sport balancing their real and often respectable lives with the possibility of a broken nose or tailbone at each game or practice. This book is at once hilarious, meticulously reported and well-written. It'll make you want to put on a pair of skates and throw an elbow. Brava to Vanstone and the people who make up the Women's Flat Track Derby Association. This book, like derby itself, is a testament to their competitive spirit."

–Jane McManus, former journalist with *ESPN*, author of *The Fast Track*

"An inspirational tale of motherhood, sisterhood and what to do with a film degree when you're an adult. Vanstone's punchy memoir is about how sometimes you need to get knocked on your ass a few times to find yourself, on and off the track."

–Sean Burns, *WBUR*, Boston

"*Don't Let Them Eat the Baby* is a lot of things: An engaging chronicle of self-discovery, and a tour through a vibrant, messy subculture. It's about ownership and agency, about messing up and trying again, falling down and getting back up. Roller derby, with its inventiveness and inclusiveness, its sense of humor and community, might be needed more now than ever. And so are stories like this about women fighting for their space in sports—and everywhere else."

–Emma Span, Enterprise Editor, *The Athletic*

"I think the coolest thing about this reflection and revelation is that roller derby has never been about making grassroots organizing a corporate gig... Derby and its members are the key holders to the proverbial kingdom."

–Jumpy McGee, a.k.a. April Fournier

DON'T LET THEM EAT THE BABY:

WHY ROLLER DERBY IS THE GREATEST SPORT NEVER SOLD

A memoirella

Erica Vanstone

Banana Pitch Press

BANANA PITCH PRESS
Copyright © 2025 by Erica Vanstone
First Edition: 2025

Library of Congress Cataloging-in-Publication Data
Title: Don't Let Them Eat the Baby / Erica Vanstone
Description: First edition. | Banana Pitch Press, 2025
Identifiers: ISBN: 979-8-9913071-5-4

Book designed by Gwendolyn Schulte at GRS Editorial, LLC
Cover art by Charlie Layton
Illustrations by Sandra Frame
Photo editing by Paul Robertson

www.bananapitch.com
Banana Pitch is a 501(c)(3)

For Trucker, Aedan, and Genny

Find yourself, then never let go.

DON'T LET THEM EAT THE BABY:

WHY ROLLER DERBY IS THE GREATEST SPORT NEVER SOLD

INTRODUCTION
by Jane McManus

Decide to play roller derby, and you have joined a secret society.

First comes the equipment; skates, pads, mouthguard, knee socks, plus miles and miles of duct tape. Then there is the language—you learn all kinds of new words that your family and friends won't understand. Rules are suspended on the track—you can break a nose or a tailbone, or have your own compromised—and no one files a legal report. Most tellingly, an acolyte might choose a new name.

So when players hear that Erica Vanstone has written a book about the sport, they might exclaim, "Who the fuck is Erica Vanstone?!"

But then you say in the language only players understand, "That's Double H, former head of the WFTDA," and you'll get a nod of recognition and respect

There is no one better positioned than Vanstone to tell the story of roller derby's resurgence through the 2010s and early '20s. She was an announcer and player for Philly Roller Derby who rose to the inner leadership circle of this unruly (and I mean that with deep affection) Women's Flat Track Derby Association, a sports league that gave voice to thousands of deeply-invested women across the world. Each of them were creating a new sports environment separate from the mono-culture around American men's sports.

During her time at the top, there were broadcast deals, a deeply-researched return to play policy during COVID, and a transgender player inclusion policy that was at first tentative and later genuinely welcoming. Each of these moves was both supported and opposed by the hundreds of vocal women and nonbinary players who pour their hearts into derby and call the track a second home. Leadership is never easy, and leading this organization requires a rare deftness that few have.

You should know, Vanstone is that kind of leader.

Once you acknowledge that the job is impossible, it becomes more fun, and Vanstone has a sunniness that makes the impossible less irritating. This book captures the spirit of derby—how fun and life-affirming it all is. How teammates become family and your life gets shaped around practice and competition.

WFTDA is a league, but the clubs couldn't be more differ-ent. Some are small and are just trying to get enough players to field two practice teams. Then you have large organizations in New York, Chicago, and Denver that have multiple levels of teams, boot camps, and junior derby. The tournaments every year have skilled teams, maybe a few Olympic-level athletes sprinkled among them, and a competitiveness that could eas-ily have mass appeal.

I first met Vanstone when I played for Suburbia Roller Derby in Yonkers as Lesley E. Visserate and was covering sports for *ESPN*, so we worked together to tell meaningful stories around the sport. In this book, she takes you into the decision-making process as a sport on the precipice of breaking through to viewers wonders what it might lose in the process.

So many of the players give so much of themselves to this community. Did it really make sense to bend it all for the approval of a traditional sports audience? Should a group of skaters who built a women's sport really soften the edges so as to avoid offending delicate sensibilities?

Vanstone tells this story with heart, perspective, and the firsthand knowledge of roller derby's history and the people who play. If you play, you'll see yourself in this book. If you don't, you may be inspired to try on a pair of skates. It is never too late, and there is a place for everyone in derby.

So, gentle reader, come along for the ride.

jam start

noun

---

the beginning of an increment of play in a roller derby game.

CHAPTER 1:

The Roller Derby Paradox

Fall, 2006. Camden, New Jersey.

Roller derby saved my soul.

These words adorn the back of a navy T-shirt on the person in front of me. I'm not sure about my soul, but my arms would appreciate a jacket in this thirty-degree weather as I wait in the parking lot of a South Jersey roller rink.

It's early December and my nose is running. It's almost too cold to smoke my cigarette in a crowd of two hundred or so people but I inhale anyway, watching lights across the river in Philadelphia blink back. Without warning, the yellow metal doors to the roller rink fly open and I'm smacked in the head by a loud crash of AC/DC. "Thunderstruck," to be exact.

"Tickets!" comes the booming voice of a woman I can't see. "Tickets, fuckers. 'f you don't have roller derby tickets, you're shit out of luck. We're sold out."

As I fumble in my jeans for the paper ticket I bought from a friend who's skating tonight, my gut grumbles. The only thing I ate today was a slice of my leftover thirtieth birthday cake to soak up the beer from last night. I take a final drag of my smoke and drop it on the frozen ground. Behind Angus Young's guitar riffs, I hear the call of something else in the background, something intangible. I step through the rink's doors and look for the friend I'm here to watch skate. My throbbing head ponders a question as I enter and look around: *So, this is roller derby?*

The rink is fluorescent and humid, tinged with the scent of burning pizza. Like me, most of the folks here are white, in their twenties and thirties. Unlike me, many of them wear fishnets or leather, tattoos and vintage red lips. I'm new to all of this. In truth, roller derby—modern roller derby—is new to most other folks here, too. Played on television in the sixties, seventies, and eighties, derby is experiencing a sort of revival, thanks to this summer's A&E reality series *Rollergirls*. Tonight in Camden, the track is flat, created by pink gaffer's tape on a wooden rink floor.

"Welcome to roller derby," a short redhead says, handing me a program with the words *Philly Roller Girls* on the cover. I take it, stepping out of the way as skaters with names like *Robin Drugstores* and *Ivana Rock* on their acid wash vests glide past me.

"*Alright ladies and germs—*" a man booms into a mic. "*Who's ready for some roller derby action?*" The announcer introduces himself as *Marcus Hook*. I can't tell which I like more, the personas in roller derby or the promise of violence on roller skates. Trying to decide, I rest my elbows on the cinder block half-wall along the rink to watch. I suddenly spot my friend who sold me the ticket—or, rather, her new persona.

"*Now jamming for the Broad Street Butchers, Persephone…*"

My friend, a petite blonde, uses the pseudonym *Persephone*, goddess of the underworld. She rolls towards the track in full roller derby gear: skates, knee pads, and a helmet. Skaters from both teams, the Broad Street Butchers, and their opponents, the Philthy Britches, sneer at one another. I can't tell if their malice is real or part of the entertainment. One of the Britches straps a helmet with a star on it over her gorgeous bald head as she approaches the track.

"Jamming for the Philthy Britches, Violet Temper..."

Violet skates over to a pink line of tape near Persephone. Both skaters crouch, ready to pounce as two referee whistles start the game. Persephone launches herself forward, past Violet and through an obstacle course of skaters. She rolls around blockers, most of them in stockings and miniskirts, and somehow remains upright, dodging hit after hit. A referee blows a whistle and aims his index finger at Persephone from the inside of the track. The crowd explodes again.

"Lead jammer!" the announcer cries.

I have no idea what *lead jammer* means, but I am invested.

Persephone makes her way alone around the entire track and sails through the pack of skaters a second time. Then, she thrusts her hands up and down at her hips, flapping like a seagull. More whistles blare. A referee in a cowboy hat holds up his right hand, wiggling all five fingers. Missy Elliot thumps from the sound system as the whole chaotic mess comes to an end.

"Five points for Persephone and the Broad Street Butchers!" Marcus Hook hollers.

"What the fuck is happening?" A man next to me about my

age throws his hands up, echoing my own perplexed sentiments. "Does anyone know how the game is played?"

I shake my head because I have no clue. Without knowing it, this frustration becomes the nexus of my journey ahead. I am confused about how roller derby works, even annoyed that I can't understand it. The crowd's frenzy only amplifies my confusion.

And yet, I am absolutely fucking smitten.

When I first found roller derby in 2006, I very much wanted it to save my soul. At the time, I was a newly married thirty-one-year-old working in the bubbling Philadelphia film industry. A coordinator on commercials, I had an NYU Film degree burning a hole in my pocket and an exhausting career working twelve hour days for stretches at a time. Unlike film school, the job was primarily pushing paperwork. Roller derby was a creative revelation.

Stepping foot in that Camden roller rink, I had no idea what I was in for. I knew what I *thought* I was in for. *Rollergirls*, the smash A&E series[1] from that previous summer, had filled my head with all kinds of wild expectations.

First, I expected to find banked track roller derby, as featured in *Rollergirls*. That version required angled platforms with padded railings, roughly a hundred feet long. TXRD Lonestar Rollergirls—later renamed Texas Roller Derby[2]—played the banked track game featured in the show. It's still what most folks think of when they hear the words *roller derby*. It's what I thought of, too. Only, when I showed up in

Camden, the track was flat.

I had also expected drama. *Rollergirls* was full of brash, cussing women fighting and skating, often poorly. Yet, they persisted on their own terms. Coincidentally, these were the same terms my own Generation X was deeply familiar with: a disaffected, not-giving-a-fuck attitude mixed with various forms of disruptive music. And beer. No wonder *Rollergirls* resonated with me.

The television show had made its way to A&E after *The Nashville Network*'s failed relaunch of a wrestling-inspired derby project under the name *RollerJam*[3] in 1999-2000. When roller derby rematerialized in Austin the following year, it was the brainchild of local musician Daniel Eduardo Policarop, otherwise known as Devil Dan.

In a recent conversation I had with flat track roller derby co-founder Amy Sherman, a.k.a. Electra Blu, she shared an anecdote I'd love to think is plausible for how Dan got the idea to begin with.

"Me and some girlfriends dressed up as a seventies roller derby team for Halloween," she recalls of the year 2000. "We skated up and down Red River District in Austin in our little seventies outfits... Later, I heard Devil Dan said he saw some girls dressed as a roller derby team, out skating, and came up with the idea to revive roller derby." Sherman laughs. "I'm not saying it was us who gave him the idea. But it was kind of a coincidence on the timing."

A *New York Times*' 2008 article[4] suggests Dan's vision probably wasn't too far off from this. "Sleeping in his car, pounding Jack Daniels and posting fliers... he managed to recruit dozens of women to a highly disorganized organizational meeting..."

Said women quickly realized Dan didn't have the means, money, or follow-through to run a roller derby of any kind. So they quickly took his idea in another direction, forming "Bad Girls Good Women"[5] productions—or the She-EOs. This group eventually formed the banked track crew I watched on *Rollergirls* in 2007. Yet when the She-EOs tried to assert ownership over roller derby, "a bunch of us left to start our own thing," shares Sherman. And that "own thing" became a global phenomenon: flat track roller derby.

When I first walked into roller derby, there was still plenty of spectacle woven into the sport, like penalty wheels. Once a skater sat in the penalty box—or, the *sin bin*—a fan would spin an actual wheel to determine a joke penalty. Like push ups or arm wrestling. Or even more degrading options like ass-smacking.

"I don't need a guy smacking my ass whenever I get a penalty" shares Sherman, referencing those early days. "A lot of us grew up playing sports," she adds, "and we wanted to... embrace our sportiness."

By the time I walked into that rink in Camden, the Texans' little sport was catching fire outside of Austin. Philly Roller Girls was one of thirty-three flat track clubs that had popped up across the country. It was sport. It was spectacle. It was like nothing I'd ever seen before.

Or, as Sherman adds, "In roller derby, I get to put on makeup and be an athlete and have this persona." This distinct cocktail is an important part of the roller derby paradox: sport and self-expression. Athletics designed for its daring participants, not for its questioning audiences. For the community, not the fan dollar.

When I first found roller derby, this allure was palpable for me. In the weeks that followed my first game, I kept coming back to the question of the man next to me: *Does anyone know how this game is played?*

I didn't know how roller derby was played, or what the hell it was, exactly. But I knew what it wasn't—conventional. And because of that, I was sold.

Not that roller derby ever gave a fuck about that either way.

Illustration by Sandra Frame,
a.k.a. Tara Armov.

drawback

verb

---

knocking a jammer out of bounds
and forcing her to re-enter the
track further back from where she
started; an offensive setback.

CHAPTER 2:

Draw Back

Winter, 2007. Philadelphia, Pennsylvania.

I'm still thinking about roller derby a few weeks later when Mark Wahlberg pokes his head in my doorway. I'm hungover in the production office of a Paramount film, where I should be ordering graphics for prop cars. Instead I'm staring at the Philly Roller Girls program. I cover it with my laptop.

"Antoine in here?" Mark asks, glancing around. I'm the only one in the production office. It takes me a second to realize he's speaking to me. Mark is stubble-cheeked, with chin-length chestnut hair and wearing mirrored sunglasses. *Right, and he's famous. There's that.*

My throat goes dry. Hair in a haphazard bun, I move a hand to cover an old coffee stain on my sweatshirt. Tasting last night's cigarettes in my mouth, I shake my head from side to side. I point down the hall in the direction of the film's director, Antoine Fuqua.

"That way," I say.

Mark nods and shuffles off down the hall. Sipping my coffee, I stretch my neck around the corner to watch him walk away. My head begins to throb.

"Make any progress on those graphics?" asks my boss of the moment as he approaches my desk. He's one of the film's art department heads, a gray, wiry man sipping pale-looking office coffee under rimmed glasses. I shake my head again; I'm supposed to be wrangling graphics for helicopters on this film. It's 8:15 a.m. and all of the places I need to call haven't opened yet.

"Just about to get on that." I put a hand over my mouth, hoping to block the beer fumes from wafting towards him. I put my coffee down next to the Philly Roller Girls program.

"Wow, what's that?" My boss grabs the program and eyes the circular logo with a roller skate in the shape of the Liberty Bell above the website URL.

"S'roller derby," I mumble, sitting down at my laptop. A production coordinator for film and television, I work long hours at this computer and on the phone, calling people and asking for things. Searching the internet. The depressing reality of my so-called creative career.

"This is sexy as hell," my boss says, flipping through pages of the roller derby program. Something about the tone of his voice makes me feel... ogled. Or, like roller derby is being ogled. I straighten as he puts it down. "Lemme know when you get those graphics."

He moves from the door and I exhale, dropping my shoulders.

Grabbing the program, I spot all kinds of tough-looking women with even tougher names: *Nina Knockout, Mo Pain, Ginger Vitis.* I realize I am not in a place yet to try out to be a roller girl. Every one of those skaters looks tough or sexy and I don't feel either of those things. But I very much want to. Sitting up in my chair I clear the search bar on my laptop and grab the Philly Roller Girls flyer. I type in the Roller Derby URL and hit Enter.

Logging on to the Philly Roller Girls website that morning, I didn't really know what I was looking for. There was a toughness combined with sexuality, a resilience that said roller derby wasn't designed for people like my boss—a slightly nerdy, older man in the film business. It felt secret, clandestine. And yet somehow out in the open. Expressions of sexuality that built power and confidence in these women.

"In roller derby, it was always okay to keep your femininity and still be a badass," derby founder Amy Sherman, a.k.a. Electra Blu, assures me in a recent chat. "In derby, it's okay to wear fake eyelashes and fishnets and still be an athlete." Yet this dichotomy was always hard for outsiders to parse. Mainly, men. Mostly because their role started as some kind of observer. Even Devil Dan and his vision of a roller derby circus was more about spectacle and fantasy. But when women took hold of the sport's management, all that changed. And quickly.

Or, as Sherman adds, "We took away spank alleys and put in real penalties."

"We wanted this sport to be ours," confirms Jennifer Wilson, a.k.a. Hydra, another Texas founder who spoke with me about its origins. "[N]o men telling us how to do it."

Though a few clubs were founded with the assistance of men—like Gotham Girls Roller Derby, co-founded by Chassis Crass and David "Lefty" Liebowitz[6]—most of the people who assembled roller derby teams were women. From business operations, to merchandise sales, to sex-positive branding, the whole sports ecosystem was constructed by de-centering men.

This didn't mean men weren't included early on. In fact, men took on the roles typically taken by women in male-centric sports: cheerleaders, fans, boosters. They also performed critical tasks like refereeing and announcing. Yet, these were supporting roles, not the main event.

Fumbling around the Philly Roller Girls website on my work laptop, I hadn't realized any of this when I felt called to learn more about roller derby. I was nerdy, analytical, and artsy; equal parts Jean-Luc Godard and Jean-Luc Picard. Like many, I was only looking to find my place. Like most, I also didn't realize I was about to find something much more important. Myself.

derby name

noun

---

a fun, campy, or pun-focused name, other than a government name, used as an identity in the roller derby community.

CHAPTER 3:

Identity Crisis

March, 2007. Feasterville, Pennsylvania.

It's 10 a.m. on a Friday, a few months later. I'm twenty miles outside of Philadelphia in the suburbs, looking around the Sportsplex, a bright, white hangar with two roller hockey rinks. And I have two problems. Well, three.

The first is that I signed up to announce a game of roller derby at this tournament on a Friday morning. I'm still moderately hung over from my regular Thursday night happy hour. Tasting last night's karaoke beer, I watch as a gaggle of girls in booty shorts and fishnets walk past with skates slung over their shoulders. I have no idea why half-sauced karaoke antics made me think I could command a room with a microphone, but in one of my braver moments, I signed up for this.

Reporting as a volunteer for Philly Roller Girls' first-ever tournament, I'm questioning my logic, pulling my red hair back into a hasty ponytail over my makeup-less face. I glance down at my beat-up brown cowboy boots with the hole at the pinky toe. I'm a fish out of water, only I'm not so sure what this water even is yet.

My second problem, which is shared by most people on the planet right now, is that I have no idea how the game of roller derby is even played. And yet, here I am, showing up on a Friday morning to talk about it. On a microphone.

The third problem arrives as my co-announcer introduces himself. "Chip Queso." He extends his hand. A roller derby legend I've heard of on the internet, Chip's just under my height, with salt-and-pepper sideburns. *Damn, I need to find a good roller derby name like his.*

I pat the hastily-scrawled *Erica* on my nametag. "I don't have a derby name yet."

"No worries, you'll find a good one," Chip says. Queso is from Texas Rollergirls, founders of the sport. And I'm more than a little intimidated by him.

Choosing a roller derby name feels so important. It has to be funny or outrageous or confident. Right now I'm none of these things. I pick up a stack of papers and eye the roster of Philly's home team, the Heavy Metal Hookers: *Felony Griffith, Val Halla, Euro Thrash.* Felony, a tall redhead, chose her name because she's on actual house arrest. I hear she wears an ankle bracelet under her socks. I tuck the top of my t-shirt into baggy jeans and reread the roster.

Minutes later, the Hookers face off against a team from Connecticut. A referee blows one short whistle and the blockers roll forward, looking over their shoulders. A second whistle starts the jammers, the point scorers behind them. Then the mass of bodies lurches counterclockwise. The Hookers' jammer, a platinum blonde with a star on her helmet, pushes through to the other side. "Lead jammer, Heavy Metal

Hookers," Queso cries into his microphone. All I can do is nod and repeat his words.

"Lead jammer," I squawk, swallowing hard. I know this means she can call off this whole mess whenever she wants to. The Hookers' jammer, wearing a green and black star, races out of the fray and around the first turn of the oval track, then the second. As she hits the straightaway, coming towards us, one of the opposing team's blockers catches up and crashes into her. She sails through the outside referee lane and slams her face down onto the floor next to me.

"You alright?" I ask, watching her crawl to her knees.

"Fuck," she says, not noticing me. Despite wearing a mouthguard, I catch the inside of her mouth, now coated in blood. A red-stained grin cracks her face as she gets up and storms back into the action. The hair on the back of my neck stands. In a good way.

This is heaven, I think. *I'm in heaven.* Not because I know what I'm looking at, but because I don't care that I don't know. And Fred Astaire's voice springs into my head, solving at least one of my problems for the day.

Roller derby names are not for your enjoyment. Alright, technically, they are. But to the community, these names are sacred; meant for our own enjoyment first and foremost. Sometimes they're chosen for fun, sometimes they're aspirational. And they're always selected to solidify a newly-emerging persona. Even if that persona changes from season to season. Finding one for myself was a rite of passage, a ritual of emergence in the community. And yet, I was struggling. One of my biggest fears when I first stepped into that skating rink to talk on a microphone was not being cool or badass enough. Something that would force me outside of any comfort zone I'd been cushioned in as an overworked, burned out film rat.

This, of course, is the magic of a derby name. The options for reinvention are endless.

Over its twenty years, modern derby has seen names shift from the wildly outlandish to the concretely inappropriate and back again. They've tackled issues of gender, racism, politics, humor, and everything in between. Yet, what's at stake in any derby name is really agency. That each of us gets to define ourselves *for ourselves*.

"I started playing roller derby when I was forty-four, and my age was always a badge of honor for me," shares The Cycrone, also known as Jocelyn Jenik, who spoke with me for this book. Jenik joined Philly Roller Girls (now, Philly Roller Derby) shortly after I did in 2007. Her own derby name combined two important concepts: "I was playing with the word 'crone,' an old, wise woman. And a cyclone is a really fast wind that goes counterclockwise."

In later years, this quest to be self-defined would act as the cornerstone of roller derby's innovative gender policies. However, in the early days of flat track, it mostly spoke to the clever badassery of its founders. Southwestern Law School professor David Fagundes explores this mystique in a 2015 article,[7] where he dissects the name of L.A. Derby Dolls banked track skater Tara Armov. Fagundes writes, "The name...suggests that Tara is tough enough that she'll tear your arm off." And anyone who knows Armov, a.k.a. Sandra Frame, can vouch for that.

"My derby name is actually a pretty boring story," Armov herself confessed to me in a recent conversation, sharing that she was batting around name ideas with her now-spouse, the aptly-named Busta Armov. "I thought of Tara Rantula because I think spiders are cool. And Busta immediately replied with Tara Armov, and that was *it*. No further discussion was needed!"

As Electra Blu's original Austin team in 2000 grew to thirty-three teams in 2007, names became increasingly important. Clubs popped up in Arizona, Minneapolis, New York, Seattle, Chicago, Philadelphia, and beyond. Electra's own name is derived from the opening lyrics from David Bowie's delicious 1977 song "Sound and Vision," and the seventies superhero show *Electra Woman and Dyna Girl*.[8] And as the sport grew, so too did disputes over names.

More and more derby names appeared that were similar, or even vaguely the same: Annie Christ vs. Auntie Christ vs. Annie Maul. Or Amanda Jamitinya vs. Amandatory Sentence. Vixen Van Go-Go vs. Vicious Van GoGo. And so on.

Around 2002, skaters from Arizona and Minnesota started a name registry called Two Evils, or the International Rollergirls Master Roster.[9] The list of derby names was designed for people to keep tabs on who's who and avoid disputes. It was maintained by Soylent Mean from Minnesota, along with Jelly HoNut and Paige Burner of Arizona.

"While derby is a serious athletic competition," Fagundes' article continues, "it is unlike most mainstream American sports in that it still manages to maintain a sense of humor about itself." This sense of humor made us even less like other women's sports at the time—an industry that was already marginalized.

A prime example was in 2010 when *ESPN* founded *espnW* and its then-Vice President Laura Gentile was quoted by the *New York Times*[10] as calling it, "'where we talk about women finding self-esteem in sports and about getting a pedicure.'"

This was crushingly the opposite of roller derby's ethos.

"In roller derby, women are out there engaging in full contact, being brassy, having fun, and having a sense of humor," says former *espnW* and *ESPN.com* writer Jane McManus. "That's a challenge to the established attitude." McManus, also a former skater for Suburbia Roller Derby in Yonkers, New York, chose her own name, Lesley E. Visserate, as an homage to one of sports broadcasting's first women, Lesley Visser.

Identity, then, is not only vital to roller derby. It's a key part of why the mainstream sports media has never quite *gotten* us. Why roller derby remains a paradox. Our fake names would ultimately become an unbridgeable chasm between us and mainstream sports media.

And maybe, just maybe, that's how it was always supposed to be. Finding what's right for us and not for anyone else. As for Erica Vanstone, she was only just figuring out what she was becoming. And who.

"Hymen Heaven."

Back at the Sportsplex in Feasterville, I extend my hand to a man in a glittering green and silver luchador mask, a sleeveless dress shirt, and a black tie. I am about to announce my second-ever roller derby game with this man, Tank from Ohio Rollergirls in Columbus.

After the Hookers game, Fred Astaire and Irving Berlin's "Cheek to Cheek" played in my head. *I'm in heaven... Hymen Heaven...* A cinephile, I thought it was clever a few hours ago. Now, I'm rethinking the reference. Looking over his biceps, muscular and covered in tattoos, I don't need to ask why my colleague chose the name Tank.

"Hymen Heaven? That's your roller derby name?" he asks.

"Yup, Hymen Heaven." My response prompts a smile that spills out from under his silvery mask. It's a bawdy name that I haven't quite parsed yet. There's a sexuality but also an innocence, a paradox. It's funny, it's cheeky. It's blush-inducing. Wiggling my toes in my boots, I feel anything but sexual. Maybe that's part of why I chose it.

"Hymen Heaven," he says. "That's awesome. You on the announcer's online chat group?" I tell him I'm not. "Mostly we talk shit and yell at each other, but you might actually learn some stuff about roller derby, too."

Tank writes the information on a piece of paper, then turns to the mic. I take the paper from him and carefully fold it, tucking it into the back pocket of my jeans like a treasure.

A buzzing comes from my pocket, my phone. *You coming home soon?*

Another hour or so! I text my husband back as the game starts.

"Alright, what's up roller derby fans? Tank comin' atcha," the announcer from Ohio says, then gives me my own microphone.

"Here with me is Philly's finest, go ahead and introduce yourself, partner."

I take a sip of warm beer and wince. It tastes like moldy socks, but I need the liquid courage as I speak into the mic. "Hey! Hey! Hymen Heaven here from Philly Roller Girls!"

For the first time, my emerging roller derby persona does the talking. She and I have only just met, but I already like the sound of her.

Referee patch, East Coast Derby Extravaganza.
Photo credit: Jen Moulton Proctor,
a.k.a. Bettie Mercury

nine-month derby injury

noun

---

when a skater becomes pregnant, delaying her skating career.

CHAPTER 4:

Of Mics and Men

June, 2007. Philadelphia, Pennsylvania.

Speaking of emerging personas, I'm suddenly two months pregnant. And I'm in a corset—and a blonde wig. These things might seem unlikely but in roller derby, we're full of paradoxes.

Another rousing Heavy Metal Hookers game is in full swing at the Sportsplex. Van Halen's "Hot for Teacher" blares while Baltimore's Charm City in black and gold racks up points against my Hookers. I still don't quite understand the game of roller derby. I rub my newly-pregnant belly, still trying to wrap my head around it. Loosening the corset's lace strings, I stand uncomfortably next to my new announcing partner.

"Eddie Spaghetti," he'd said when I met him a few minutes ago. "Gefilte Fists' boyfriend." Fists is a short, muscular skater for the Philthy Britches. She stands nearby looking cute and comfortable in red booty shorts. Tall, with spiked brown hair, Eddie carries the hint of a Carolina drawl and wears gray leopard print pants. He's relaxed, laid back. Whereas I feel like an anxious sausage stuffed into a too-tight skin.

Seeing Eddie and Fists, I'm reminded of my own husband at home. He's not into derby, which is fine; we don't have to do everything together. Still, I'm impressed at how many partners are here, including the one on the mic next to me.

"Whiplash on the jammer line for the Hookers," Eddie says into the mic.

The next pack of Hookers take the track and the DJ drops Iron Maiden. Blocker Ivana Rock pulls a black and white bandana up over her face, like she's about to rob a bank. Crouching, she flashes a two-part tattoo with the words *Heavy* and *Metal* in cursive ink on the backs of her thighs.

Two dozen or so family members and spectators applaud around the track. Men who look like boyfriends and husbands linger trackside near the benches for Charm City. Their mascot, a man in a felt banana costume, high-fives two drag queens standing trackside in sequined dresses.

A whistle sounds and Ivana joins Euro Thrash, Robin Drugstores, and Val Halla in forming a wall, creating a barrier to keep Charm's jammer behind them. A second whistle sounds and the Hookers' jammer, Wendy Whiplash, with long, snaking dreadlocks, squeezes through an opening between Baltimore's skaters. A referee in the middle of the track points at her and makes two sharp whistle blasts. *Oh, I know what this is!*

"Lead jammer, Wendyyyyyy Whiplash," I growl into the mic. This means she can call off the jam at any time. Whiplash uses powerful legs to hustle around the eighty-foot track then sails through the wall of blockers one more time. She flaps her hands against her hips.

"Four points and a call off for Whiplash and the Hookers," I say, as a series of four short whistles ring in a row to end the jam.

"That's *five* points, Hymen," Eddie says, correcting me on the mic. "Don't forget that pesky jammer lap point." He gestures to Charm's jammer, who was still trapped in the pack. Heat floods my face. Whiplash not only got the points for passing Charm's blockers, she got a fifth point for passing their jammer.

"Ah, you're right, Eddie," I say, trying to think fast. "That's because Whiplash was so lightning-fast that I missed half of her pass through the pack." I'm learning how to turn mistakes into opportunities. Just as important, I'm learning how this wild, raucous game works.

So how, exactly, do you play the game of roller derby? By the time 2007 rolled around, nearly everyone discovering roller derby was asking this exact question. Founded in 2005, the Women's Flat Track Derby Association (WFTDA) attempted to answer it.

The ten or so clubs that started flat track roller derby—teams like Texas, Arizona, and Seattle—formed a loose online collective, the United Leagues Coalition (ULC). Folks from the ULC used online workgroups to create a common rule set and officiating standards. In 2005, a handful of ULC members met in Chicago and the WFTDA was formed. Juliana Gonzales, a.k.a. Bloody Mary, was in the room for its birth.

Gonzales confides in a recent chat with me, "We were just

focused on rules and standards." These rules and standards are likely first of their kind designed exclusively by women. "We split up the table of contents and each of us wrote a section. Over the next couple months, that's how the WFTDA and a flat track roller derby rule set was built."

This remarkable thirty-two-page rule set was the first of its kind and boasted a simple yet radical motto: *By the skaters. For the skaters. Always.*

The rules were equally revolutionary and modern, a host of regulations pulled partially from banked track, partially from several months of playing a unique flat track game. All with one important goal: to score points.

"A jammer's role is to make her way through the pack, lap the pack, and pass through the pack as many times as she chooses in a jam to score points for her team," states the 2007 edition of *Women's Flat Track Derby Association's Standardized Flat Track Roller Derby Rules.*[11]

In a nutshell, this is the game of roller derby: a jammer scores points by passing the hips of opponents. Blockers from an opposing team are trying to stop her. That's it. That's the game.

Banked track had always taken a more flamboyant license, one that was also steeped in challenging gender dynamics. Or, as Electra Blu shares, "that version of roller derby often featured co-ed games or teams... but [audiences] wanted cat fights from the women."

Such "cat fights" were developed by a man named Jerry Seltzer. In his 2019 *New York Times* obituary, the late roller derby promoter was called a visionary for developing a game with "two teams of five helmeted players muscling, elbowing, kicking, shoving and tossing each other while circling a banked track counterclockwise."

Though his father, Leo Seltzer, created roller derby as an endurance contest on roller skates in the 1920s and thirties,[12] Jerry's iteration of the sport became a sensation in the 1960s. Seltzer and I never saw eye-to-eye on a lot of things. But one of the areas we always closely aligned on was the importance—though, not always the execution—of gender representation in sports. Spotting roller derby's revival in the early 2000s, Seltzer reached out to the WFTDA early on—a move that elicited mixed feelings from its feminist founders.

Bloody Mary recalls of their early exchanges: "Seltzer was promoting a very different, objectifying, sexist, entertainment-oriented product, versus what we were trying to do." What Bloody and others *did* align with was Seltzer's belief that roller derby could be big—so much bigger than it was. Even if it was misunderstood. Even if it was birthed by women who were only just starting to understand what womanhood even meant. In sport and elsewhere.

As Hymen Heaven and flat track roller derby are finding our voices, I hear my own screams echoing into the quiet whirring of a small delivery room. I'm in labor. After months of growing and waiting, I'm in a hospital bed, knees bunched up to my chest. A six-inch epidural needle rests on a tray next to me—a sight that would normally make my skin crawl. Now, it means relief as I grip the bed. I've never experienced pain like this before, a searing hotness like I'm splitting in half. It's otherworldly, almost ethereal. My husband rubs his eyes.

"One more push, Erica," my OBGYN says and I bear down. A mirror next to her reveals the top of my son's head coming out of my own body. As I take a breath he gets sucked back inside of me. Disheartening, demoralizing. Exhausting.

"I can't." I feel hot tears on my face. "I can't do this anymore."

"Yes, you can." She's laughing at me as I shake my head in disbelief.

My husband, who has gotten more rest than I have, scratches the top of his bald head and shifts from side to side. He reaches for my hand but I squeeze down on the morphine instead.

"Can't I just rest for a few minutes?" *Or another hour?*

She laughs. "Come on. You're stronger than you think you think you are."

Am I really? I'm not sure. I resolve to end this brief window of pain, to take on yet another identity completely unknown to me: *Mom.* Taking a deep breath, I bear down to the sound of my doctor cheering me on: "You got this, Mama."

eat the baby

verb

---

when a jammer is knocked out of bounds, dragged backwards a full lap around the track, and captured by the opposing blockers.

CHAPTER 5:

The Mothership

March, 2008. Philadelphia, Pennsylvania.

Months after the birth of my son, I'm back on the mic next to Eddie Spaghetti at the 23rd Street Armory, a warehouse space in Center City, Philadelphia, where the Army stores tanks during times of peace. As a blocker for the Broad Street Butchers sends a skater flying off the track, I know this roller derby game is anything but a time of peace.

"Massive hit from Mary That Motha Oh God, taking down Felony Griffith," Eddie hollers into his mic

"But you can't keep a Hooker down long, can you, Eddie?" I add.

"Not until they've been paid," he quips back after a guffaw. His statement makes me spit-take the water I'm sipping off mic. The appropriateness of our remarks is doubtful. The energy? Electric. Derby announcers have developed a culture of pushing the envelope like this. Sometimes we rip it clear in half. We aren't just narrators, we're shaping the game as we go, the culture. I'm not thinking, I'm just enmeshed in this wild energy.

"Three more points for the Butchers," I holler as the jam comes to a natural conclusion, resolving in four whistle blasts. DJ Vixen Van Go Go drops "I Love Rock and Roll" by Joan Jett. An ache in my nursing bra reminds me I have other priorities waiting at home.

Everyone in my little family is trying to find a new normal. For me, this looks like pumping enough milk to announce roller derby games, running out for four or so hours once a month. I can't wait until my kid is old enough to be here, but for now, roller derby is a breather from motherhood for a few hours.

Fans holler in the bleachers, holding red plastic cups of beer and lifting signs with slogans like, "*Butcher Them Butchers!*" and "*Hail Skatin'!*"

On the jammer line for the Butchers, Persephone, also a new mom, waits for her whistle, then immediately knocks the Hookers' jammer, Mandawar, out of bounds. Persephone intentionally skates backwards. To avoid a penalty, Mandawar has to re-enter behind Persephone, so Mandawar has no choice but to keep going back. A game within a game, a tactic called *eating the baby*. It's a term that makes me squirm. I'm not sure I'd like to contemplate eating any babies. Yet, I'm reminded of my own son's head retreating back into my womb between pushes during childbirth. Though, I admit *reabsorb the baby* doesn't have the same ring.

"Looks like we're about to *eat the baby*, Hymen," Eddie says into the mic. Persephone skates all the way back, a full lap around to meet the front of her wall of blockers. She motions to her teammates to move up and capture Mandawar as they reenter the track.

"A strategy only a mother could love," I add. The roar of the crowd makes my heart soar as the Butchers trap Mandawar. Persephone circles back to grab points before calling it off, flapping hands to her hips. The game is starting to make sense to me. And I love it.

"Big win on that jam for the Butchers, Eddie!" I howl into the mic. The crowd agrees.

Next up, Robin Drugstores is on the jammer line for the Heavy Metal Hookers. Her daughter, Fire Unicorn, runs up and down the side of the track with green pom poms. Before the game, I'd watched the girl pretend to spray her mother with invisible magic for good luck. I can only hope to have my son here in the same way one day. The jam begins.

Eddie and I lean into the game's big hits and plays, bantering with each other and then the crowd. We are preachers in this church of derby. Not the main event, just the gateway to it. Orators, mediators of a divine feminine flat track energy. Milk and honey in a barren sports landscape. And man, are these souls thirsty.

Some of my favorite mothers were Hookers. I realize how this sounds but it's true. Heavy Metal Hookers like the Cycrone and Robin Drugstores—and skaters just like them in clubs around the country—were inadvertently normalizing motherhood as part of a sports environment.

"The only reason I even thought about trying out for roller derby was Drugs," says the Cycrone, a.k.a. Jocelyn Jenik. A widow and mother of two young boys at the time, Jenik cites Robin Drugstores—also a single mom—as her main inspiration for putting on skates in 2007. "Drugs and I, we were already arranging joint babysitting. We lived blocks away from each other… so we would trade off or bring the kids with us to practice."

To give some perspective around how revolutionary this was at the time, not even the WNBA, the first professional women's sports league, allowed paid family leave after childbirth until 2022. Yet, in roller derby—and probably because the sport was amateur—if a skater needed to bring in her kids to practice, most clubs allowed it. Often, this meant collaborating with teammates, as Jenik did, to pool childcare solutions.

In a 2010 interview she did with *Inside Press*,[13] former *ESPN* writer and Suburbia Roller Girls skater Jane McManus shared: "'Kids love watching their mothers do something powerful.' …kids know all about the constraints on crying in case mommy is knocked off her bearings. 'They know it's part of the game,' [McManus] says.'"

"Juggling the demands of parenthood with those of a… sports career is just one of myriad challenges female athletes face," journalist Anna Furman writes in a May 2023 *Associated Press*[14] article. Roller derby not only recognized these challenges, it wove them into the strong fabric of the community.

"I have a fourteen-month-old baby," shares former London skater Kitty Decapitate, a.k.a. Kristen Lee, in a 2017 interview with the WFTDA.[15] "We train three times a week, and that means it's essentially like a full night out because of… how long it takes to get there in London."

With or without partners, many women spent time carving a new persona for themselves in the sport, only to find their image shifting yet again with motherhood. Or, as I discovered, both personas often emerged at the same time. My own son's arrival forced me to reevaluate my film career; I knew there was no way both my husband and I would be able to work twelve-hour days with an infant, so I became a temporary stay-at-home mom who volunteered in roller derby.

For many, it was a perfect storm for conflicting identities.

"I struggled with the idea of being a mom," adds Kitty. "I wanted to be Kitty the roller derby player... but I knew that I was becoming something else." That *something else* was a role many of us couldn't see until it was already formulating.

An hour or so after the double header at the Armory, I take myself and my leaking bra home to find my infant son crying in his father's arms. The sound of it makes my chest ache—a biology I can't control in a body wildly unfamiliar to me.

The two sit watching a rebroadcast of an earlier golf game. The boy is teething. I take him from his dad's arms and pull him close. We rock together, back and forth as I nurse. He closes his eyes.

"D'you eat?" I ask my husband.

"Yeah, there's pizza left in the kitchen 'f' you want." He rises to go to the bathroom and a sudden pang of guilt makes my stomach hurt. I inhale, eyeing my husband's can of beer. It's been months since I've touched one myself—mostly because I'm too tired. And also because I quit smoking. My son squeezes his hand in my face.

I am new to motherhood, yet I wouldn't trade it for the world. Being a wife feels less rewarding—at least, less rewarding than, say, the role of roller derby announcer. Or film production coordinator. Derby and motherhood, though, crackle with possibility.

Robin Drugstores.
Photo credit: Philly Roller Derby
and Heavy Metal Hookers.

zebra

noun

---

slang term for an official.

CHAPTER 6:

(Derby) Girls on Film

Fall, 2008. Portland, Oregon.

"Anything is possible, fans. This is still anybody's game." It's November and I have a microphone in my hand for the final day of *Northwest Knockdown*, the 2008 WFTDA Championships in Portland, Oregon. It's months after my game at the Armory and I'm talking to three thousand people on a microphone. *Three thousand.*

A year ago, I was fumbling to find a derby name for myself. Today, I'm sweating through a charcoal blazer in front of thousands. I glance to the side of the track and see my one-year-old son guzzling a bottle in his stroller with Persephone's husband. My own husband is working back in Philly; I'm not sure if he'd call derby announcing "work," but I do.

Here at *Northwest Knockdown*, things are crisp and exciting. Third place in the 2008 WFTDA Championships is on the line. Philly's new All Stars team, the Liberty Belles, are bringing the hammer down on the Texas Rollergirls' Texecutioners, with a score of 73-60. Dressed in black and red uniforms, the *Texies* are doing something they don't normally do —they're losing. To my Liberty Belles.

"Still anybody's game," I repeat, turning to Jim "Koolaid" Jones, my Austin-based co-announcer. He's a Texas ER nurse with a bass-filled voice, Chip Queso's counterpart.

"If, by 'anybody's game' you mean *anybody from a state south of the Mason-Dixon*, then yes, this is still *anybody's game*, Hymen," he jokes, letting me know I can't count Texas out yet.

Looking at the crowd, I also spot something oddly familiar: film equipment. I count at least four cameras, including a jib arm. I've heard sports network MavTV brokered a deal with Rose City Rollers and Seattle's Rat City Rollergirls, the Championships hosts, to broadcast this event. Only, something about the camera layout seems off to me. The cameras chased the action like they were covering NASCAR. *Those cameras are panning too fast*, I think.

"Philly fans, let's hear it for our Liberty Belles," I holler into the microphone. Near-full bleachers of cheering fans vibrate back in my direction. I've never been connected to an audience of this size before and I am jolted by its life force.

Only, I can't stop looking at those cameras; how they appear to be chasing the action instead of allowing it. I feel like I want to say something about it. But who would I even talk to? I'm just some new girl on the mic. *Hymen Heaven*. Who am I to recommend that anything change in a sport like roller derby?

MavTV's presence represented a huge step towards so-called mainstream visibility. Yet no one knew how to film roller derby. Not even us.

"By the time I became Executive Director of the WFTDA in 2009, we were experiencing this onslaught of being approached with deals of all kinds," says Juliana Gonzales, a.k.a. Bloody Mary, talking about how the internet progressed visibility of the sport. "Broadcast, marketing, publicity—all kinds of outside deals."

Teams like Minnesota RollerGirls, Carolina Rollergirls, and Gotham Girls Roller Derby were all producing their own streaming videos, posting them online for folks around the country to watch. The WFTDA left them alone—mostly because the organization was more concerned with standardizing the rules.

Bloody Mary adds, "We knew nothing about how to manage broadcast deals, what a good deal was, what a bad deal was." MavTV was a little of both. Good for the exposure, bad because no one at a network knew how to film roller derby yet.

"Granted, it was not on *ESPN* or even *Lifetime*," Kristin Seale, a.k.a. Mercy Less, shared on public-facing news site *Derby News Network*.[16] "[But] we had to get a jump on the public's image of our fledgling sport, before someone did something crazy to it."

Derby News Network,[17] or *DNN*, was an early roller derby blog and media site, the sport's first endemic media company. Other homegrown media outlets began to pop up, and all of these grassroots efforts—zines, podcasts, volunteer streams—helped grow the sport faster than the WFTDA could keep up with.

So, by the time *Northwest Knockdown* came around, MavTV[18] aired it alongside American Motorcyclist Association (AMA) and other niche wheel-based sports. In designing their coverage for *Northwest Knockdown*, the producers clearly took cues from racing, which I hated immediately. And Mav's roller derby deal wasn't cheap: according to *DNN*,[19] the network invested close to $500,000 in *Northwest Knockdown*. Watching from the sidelines as a brand new announcer, the filmmaker in me felt it was a lot of money to spend on something no one seemed to understand. I wondered: *How does mainstream sports really see roller derby, anyway?*

Northwest Knockdown.
Photo credit: Philly Roller Derby.

official review

noun

---

a time out to ask officials to review
an action in the previous jam.

CHAPTER 7:

Almost Famous

December, 2008. Philadelphia, Pennsylvania.

It doesn't take me long to learn what mainstream sports thinks of roller derby. A month or so later, I'm back home in Philly watching MavTV's rebroadcast of *Northwest Knockdown* on my computer. A male broadcaster I've never seen before, likely one of MavTV's go-to anchors, yuks it up as he watches a skater go by.

"There's a lot of hot girls here to hit on, bro." He utters this sentence, and any hope I had that roller derby was understood by MavTV is completely dashed. And it gets worse as I hear the network slogan: "For men, by men.... about the ladies."

My son hiccups and I remember I'm burping him. I pat his back while sitting at my desk. Mothering is still my full-time job and I'm alone in the middle of the day. In between cartoons, I head to my computer to watch derby.

MavTV's production is chaotic. It has high quality cameras and graphics, but the shots make no sense. As suspected, it's turn after turn of skaters rolling forward towards the camera, like in car racing. With NASCAR, this works because the track is huge, longer than most city blocks. With roller derby, the track is compressed and the camera keeps panning non-stop. It's dizzying to watch.

MavTV did end up using some announcers from roller derby—even my own voice made it into some of the weekend's videos. But the not-so-thinly-veiled misogyny framed by the uneducated producers makes all that a moot point in my mind. A few nasty comments my fellow announcers have posted in our online chat group echo this sentiment.

A cable network can't do better than this?

I can do a better broadcast for way less.

None of these skaters would let you hit on them… "bro."

My son coughs and I bounce him on my knee.

"I know, it's horrible, isn't it?" I ask him and he mashes my face with his chubby little fingers. "We can do better than this, can't we, kid?"

I'm a mother and I love everything about being a mother—save for the part where I'm alone most of the day. Still, I'm a filmmaker. A dreamer. A lover of good storytelling. In my mind, I keep going back to those cameras and how they whipped back and forth following the action. I don't know what I would do differently, I just know that it would be better than this.

I was starting to see an idea. I only needed to figure out how to articulate it.

Heading into 2009, I was far from the only filmmaker in roller derby. The fact that roller derby existed in film production hubs like New York, Los Angeles, and soon, Philadelphia, meant, by default, there were people in the industry involved. Even clubs in the Carolinas and Minnesota got in on broadcast, often through their venues.

"2005 was the NHL player's strike," shares Jeremy Stomberg, a.k.a. Minnesota RollerGirls' John Maddening. "The River Center complex… is owned by the city of St. Paul. They said, 'we have a bunch of dates to fill because we don't know if there's hockey.' And one of the things that got us was the use of their professional photographers and editing software. The same people who did Minnesota Wild games were suddenly operating our cameras."

Both Minnesota and Gotham had early access to professional resources; both clubs were using these resources to showcase roller derby using totally different camera angles and looks. It was clear that clubs around the country wanted greater exposure. Only, the folks didn't have one uniform way to showcase the sport.

Similarly, independent media sites like *Derby News Network* were streaming with resources they had available. My biggest issues with their model were inconsistencies like spotty internet, camera placement, and volunteer camera operators.

I saw an opportunity to take all the bits of broadcast theory, to gather all of these ideas and develop a common look and feel, with announcers who explained the game. Besides, if the WFTDA could create a collective rule set or standards across the sport, why couldn't we also build and manage our own broadcasts? After all, Major League Baseball was doing it.

Around 2002, MLB had decided to produce its own

broadcasts with MLB.tv. I wasn't thinking roller derby could do anything on the scale of MLB. But it was such a bold, rogue move to walk away from major networks in favor of starting a branded independent channel.

ESPN had also just started its own streaming enterprise, an experimental online channel geared towards bringing in smaller, less well-known live sports content. Established in 2005, *E+*, known then as *E360.com*[20] and later *ESPN3*, "was a chance to show other sports that would have never had the chance to be seen," according to former *ESPN* Director of Programming and Acquisitions, Todd Myers.

Building a dedicated streaming program for the WFTDA made good sense. The more I talked to folks, the more something clicked for me—and unknowingly, it was also clicking for Bloody Mary, the WFTDA, and others around the derbysphere. Maybe "by the skaters, for the skaters" could apply to broadcasts, too?

"What about video streaming ECDX this year?" I say absent-mindedly, almost as though I expect no one to listen to me.

It's January 2009 and I'm at The Cycrone's house in South Philly at a Philly Roller Girls planning meeting. She's a few years older than me; both of her boys are older than my son, but they generously share a boxful of Legos that captivate him. I watch as my toddler fixates on a green block while the dozen or so skaters in the room ponder the upcoming season.

"Ooh, streaming," says Euro Thrash, a Heavy Metal Hooker with a public relations background. Her long blonde hair pulled back in a neon green bandana, she nods her head in agreement. "That could be a good way to get people to come."

"How do you get people to come if they're home watching the stream?" another Hooker says with a scowl.

"It's great marketing," adds a lanky skater with the number ninety-nine tattooed on her arm.

"Sounds expensive," another says.

"Maybe not," I say, handing my son a small square of pita bread. "Carolina Rollergirls has a volunteer who does it. They're coming this year, right?' The Cycrone reads the list of confirmed teams on her laptop aloud, which includes both Carolina and Gotham. Both organizations have regular internet streams.

"I could reach out to them and see if we can put something together that's more of a shoestring budget?" I suggest. *Roller derby-led streaming.* It's coming together in my mind.

Without missing a beat, Cycrone responds. "What we need is a *skate lace* budget."

"You got a budget for that?" Thrash asks.

"I can make one," I say as my son chomps on his piece of pita. I hand him a sippy cup hybrid with apple juice and he slurps at it. "I bet we could get it done with mostly volunteers." I don't have this all fully formed in my head, not yet. A few volunteers, maybe some borrowed gear. A headset or two. And a vague notion that if roller derby can make its own rules, its own sport, why not its own setup for broadcast? What do we have to lose in trying?

"Failure is good. We like failure," says Three Dollar Bill, the volunteer video wrangler from Carolina Rollergirls, as he replaces a BNC cable on the video camera in front of him. Just under six feet tall, with sandy brown hair and glasses, he smirks as he switches out the cable.

Months after sitting in The Cyclone's living room, I'm standing on the mezzanine at the East Coast Derby Extravaganza. It's June, and Bill and I, along with some camera operators from Gotham, are pushing out a stream on *Derby News Network*. Philly is hosting Championships this fall—and I'd love to use this weekend to work out some of the kinks.

"There's data in failure," Bill says, clarifying his earlier point. "That's what I meant, Hymen. Failure teaches you how to avoid more failure."

"Does it? Couldn't we just do the failure-avoiding from the beginning?"

He grins, ignoring my question as he adds a score overlay, pulled from a long wire leading to the officials sitting at the tables below us—a system he helped configure called the *Carolina Scoreboard*. Bill hits a button and the monitor shows one of our camera angles with a rudimentary score overlay.

An ache at my bra line lets me know it's time to pump milk again soon. My kid is almost a year and a half old and with his grandparents this weekend while I play roller derby producer. I know that soon I'll wean my boy, a bittersweet shift on the horizon. Bill hands me a headset so I can listen to Eddie Spaghetti and Hitman Hank from Connecticut on the nearby track. I watch the program feed going out on the internet: a three-camera layout featuring a hero shot from the mezzanine.

One of the skaters waves to the camera at turn four as she heads to the track.

"Can't quite see who's jamming, Hank," Eddie says. I panic. Looking around, I see a nearby program and grab it. I open it to the team's roster and hand it to Eddie, who smiles and says, "Looks like that's number eighty nine…" as he searches for the skater's name.

I need to make sure announcers have rosters, I think as I look up again. From where we're standing, it's hard to see the track well. And the monitor isn't showing the skater either. Bill's setup is akin to MavTV's, only at a higher angle and with a lower budget. The camera angles are decent, the broadcast announcers are clear. Yet the shots together don't make the action easy to follow. It's coming together, but it's not where I want it to be. Not quite.

What Bill, *DNN*, and other community streamers saw as a way to make sure folks around the world could see games, I was slowly coming to see as my *purpose*: creating a way to share roller derby's brazen, feminist glory with the world. A way to not just take up space but claim it in a masculine sports landscape. I can feel this as I peer at Bill's setup.

"Not convinced?" He asks. "Camera angles? Scoreboard? Yes? No?"

"Not yet. But close," I say. Close enough to feel we're on the verge of something. Something much bigger than me; much bigger than all of us.

whip

noun

---

when a blocker allows a jammer to pull or "whip" a skater around her; often using a hand grab or uniform pull.

CHAPTER 8:

Whip It!

November, 2009. Philadelphia, Pennsylvania.

Bloody Mary looks intimidating as hell. Her ice blue eyes latch onto me as I stand in the Texas Rollergirls locker area, a concrete square lined in black pipe-and-drape at the back of the Pennsylvania Convention Center hall. We're both here for the 2009 WFTDA Championships, *Declaration of Derby*, hosted by Philly. She's bent down tying her laces and tilts her head at me. I take a deep breath and ask the question I've been longing to ask her in person for a few months.

"What would you think of starting a WFTDA broadcast channel?" Everything else—officiating, rules, events—is done under the WFTDA umbrella. Why not broadcast?

Bloody Mary rises and says with a scoff, "I can barely get the WFTDA to agree on calling penalties the same way." Her point is well made. Earlier in the weekend, I attended an hour-long meeting on how to call one penalty. To say these are formative days in the sport is an understatement.

"Alright, then how much longer do you want to deal with weird sexist dudes making content about us?" I ask, feeling that somehow, what I was really pitching was a world where we didn't have to be explained by men. "With camera angles that make no sense?"

"That's more my concern," she says. "Quality. Consistency."

Across the track, I see a Philly skater hanging a poster for the new Drew Barrymore movie *Whip It*. The art shows a tentative-looking jammer in a green uniform and helmet cover. The movie just came out, and it tells the story of a rookie skater whose life changes through roller derby. A story of reinvention, of change. Of aforementioned soul-saving. But it also features banked track, a fact that only blurs flat track even further. People come to flat track expecting, as I did, to see something else. I feel the weight of this pressure as I talk to Bloody.

"So, what if the broadcast and the rights were all owned and managed by the WFTDA?" I ask. Then, I grow bolder. "By *us*?" That I include myself in this statement is probably not lost on Bloody Mary because she grins.

"So, you'd be willing to take this on, then?" She asks. "As a volunteer?"

I feel a buzzing in my pocket and look at my cell phone. *What time are you done?* It's my husband texting. I don't answer. Instead, I turn back to Bloody.

"Look, I'm a mom with a film degree burning a hole in my pocket. I feel like this is my little corner of expertise. I'd be happy to take this on as a volunteer."

Looking across the convention hall, the atmosphere is exhilarating and abuzz with expectation for the weekend. A handful of volunteers rearrange pieces of the sport court. Here,

I'm not just needed, I'm valued. At home, I'm *cooking, cleaning, cartoons, repeat.* As Bill says, there's data in failure. I'm just not sure how much more of it I can stomach.

"Alright," Bloody says, pulling on her helmet. "I need a broadcast proposal."

I can't believe what I am hearing but I respond, "Abso-fucking-lutely."

By the time I met her in a convention hall in Philadelphia, Juliana Gonzales had been the Executive Director of the 501c3 WFTDA for only a few months. What I didn't see at the time but came to understand, was that in our own ways, we were both trying to carve out something critical in roller derby: agency.

One of Bloody's main goals was to try to wrangle in all of the explosive growth that was happening in roller derby. She saw immediately the need for a unified brand for flat track. *Whip It* and MavTV had only amplified that urgency. The film *Whip It,* based on the book *Derby Girl*[21] by L.A. skater Shauna Cross, had gotten a lot of eyes on roller derby in recent weeks—despite the fact that the film and book were about banked track.

"We started to make it clear to people that leagues had to ask [the WFTDA's] permission to put deals and projects together," says Gonzales of our first meeting. "So that some small league wasn't making decisions for the whole of roller derby."

Between *Rollergirls*, MavTV, and *Whip It,*[22] roller derby had been overwhelmed by other people's visions of the sport. As WFTDA Executive Director, Gonzales ran into a whole host of concerns around standardizing the sport. For example, roller derby leagues contracted with the United States Association of Roller Sports, or USARS,[23] for insurance. A branch of the International Olympic Committee (IOC), USARS was the governing body for speed skating, artistic skating, and any other sport on eight wheels. They also offered insurance to roller derby.

Up until 2009, USARS had only ever insured non-contact roller sports. Most roller derby clubs were skating in roller rinks, spaces where speed skating and artistic skating were already happening. So WFTDA approached USARS for insurance. Then, when injuries began to pile up, USARS wasn't pleased.

As I was tackling camera layouts, Gonzales was navigating how to make roller derby insurable—a pressing issue. Yet as a jammer for the Texecutioners, Bloody also knew sport ownership was becoming important. Even if that ownership was mostly perception.

"For me," shares Bloody, "that's a core part of what WFTDA became—protecting our collective images and likenesses." If the WFTDA had ownership over the sport, it would force all of these individual dealmakers to one, unified table.

Broadcast was a natural way to stake that claim, to retain ownership of the sport. To protect what women like Bloody, Electra, Hydra, and others had created. Something *by the skaters, for the skaters*. Even if I wasn't exactly a skater. Or if what it meant to *be* a skater was changing.

runt

verb

---

when a blocker is picked off intentionally to reform the pack; also called a "goat."

CHAPTER 9:

Game Changer

November, 2009. Philadelphia, Pennsylvania.

"Tannibal Lector, she likes her jammers with a nice Chianti."
Randy Pan the Goat Boy says this as Olympia's Oly Rollers
crush Texas. It's the final game of the 2009 Championships
and his reference to *Silence of the Lambs* makes me chuckle.
But the sentiment is spot on: Oly's defense, led by heavy-hit-
ting blockers like Tannibal Lector and Hockey Honey, is killer.

Oly's created an unexpected turn of events—a series of wins
over every team they've played this weekend. A Cinderella
story featuring this little-known team from Olympia,
Washington. And Philly loves a good underdog.

Derby News Network is carrying the stream using some of
my camera placements. I also have two cameras along the
straightaway, and one placed at Turn One—the first turn
after the jammer line. I'm standing next to Randy Pan and
Corndog, pointing at the roster and passing them notes every
so often. We're running a test announcing setup. I scribble on
a scrap of paper and hand it to Corndog: *What does Texas need
to come back from this?*

"Texas jammers need to find some daylight, here," says Gotham's Corndog, reading and nodding. He explains that Oly's relentless defense is almost too much for Texas. The fact that a team from the middle of the Pacific Northwest has gotten Texas' number speaks to the growing popularity—and importance—of streaming video. Olympia is the first team to have this kind of success using video to learn the game. Their jammers come from speed skating, hockey, and figure skating; they're fast and versatile, and it shows in the score, now 134–98.

An Oly skater stands from the bench and yells into the crowd.

"Oly, Oly, Oly!" the skater screams. A collective response comes from the bleachers, a sound that lights up the Pennsylvania Convention Center. Earlier in the weekend, Denver's team tried slowing Oly down but couldn't hold them. Now, Texas looks exhausted, mostly because Oly has been able to outrun or out block them.

Olivia Shootin' John, a.k.a. OJ, gets lead jammer for Texas, but she's quickly reabsorbed by opposing blockers in the pack. There's no way Texas can make up the more than fifty points they need in the seconds they have left.

"Cinderella has had an amazing time at the ball, and did not turn back into a pumpkin," Corndog announces as the clock winds down, pointing to Oly's fairytale performance, with a 178–100 win at the 2009 WFTDA Championships. He turns to nod at me, a look that tells me he probably feels the same as I do: *Holy shit, an upset.*

Upsets aren't only good for me and broadcast, they're good

for roller derby. Unexpected outcomes build intensity and suspense. I'm not sure Texas would agree as the Oly Rollers gather in the middle of the track and hoist the WFTDA's Championship trophy above their heads, a heavy metal roller skate on a giant pewter pedestal called *The Hydra*. Named after the founding skater from Texas, Jennifer Wilson, The Hydra is now headed to Olympia, Washington.

So, as the cameras catch a humble victory, what I see is how sport beats spectacle. And I'm determined to figure out a way to showcase that.

"Oly/Texas, that was *the* bout," says Corndog, underscoring my own feelings about *Declaration of Derby* in 2009. "In my opinion, at least—that was the bout that changed roller derby. Gotham had been trying to figure out how to deal with Texas. In fact, most teams were worried about Texas. So to see a team come out who had obviously watched tape, and Texas not being able to react fast enough, was incredible."

And this was the critical point: Oly was proof that roller derby streaming was not only *reaching* people around the world, it was *teaching* people around the world. Reviewing video of your opponents is a critical part of other sports—and this is one paradigm shift that materialized at *Declaration of Derby*. Olympia, Denver, and others had leveraged the influx of roller derby streams to their advantage by simply watching and learning. Seemingly overnight, we had ourselves a national sport.

How had it not only taken off, but accelerated into a

competitive sport so quickly? In my mind, modern roller derby exploded for three main reasons: the game's ease and affordability of setup, internet and broadcast, and outside media coverage driving people to find us.

First, flat track's playing surface was easy to lay down.

"We wanted something you could set up anywhere," says Amy Sherman, co-founder of the sport and designer of the original—and official—flat track.[24] "We looked at the banked track and flattened it," Sherman tells me. "And I said, well a perfect circle won't work because of physics… I had AutoCAD, which I used to pull it into an oval."

Sherman's layout established what was at one time the fastest growing sport in the world.[25] With relatively few materials—chalk, a tape measure, a roll of gaffer's tape, and some rope—anyone could make a flat track. Banked tracks, conversely, were "upwards of twenty grand at the time, more now," Sherman adds.

Yet in 2009, it was clear *Whip It* had driven more people to learn about flat track, even though we weren't featured in the movie. The film captured pop culture and mainstream media's attention—though, from a box office perspective, the film was considered a flop. *L.A. Times* writer Joe Flint[26] chalks this up to the very same problem roller derby itself encounters—the paradox of identity.

"[*Whip It*] opened at $4.6 million and fell fast…There seems to have been some confusion as to whether the movie is a sports flick, hipster flick, or a chick flick. In reality, it is a little of all three…" Nailing roller derby down as any one of these is also impossible.

To outsiders, roller derby remained synonymous with spectacle, even as we were deep in the throes of birthing a sport. The moments I witnessed at Oly vs. Texas in 2009 were unknowingly the imprint of a supernova; a quiet snapshot of this explosive turning point.

Skaters, photographers, officials, and announcers left the game feeling simultaneously excited—and like we had so much work to do to keep this momentum. And the complexity of it told me it was much more than spectacle. Roller derby, without a doubt, was a sport. And I was on a quest to find the best tools to make sure everyone knew it.

Minnesota Roller Derby (Girls) Storm Trooper
Penalty Box, circa 2009.
Photo credit: Paul Robertson/Preflash Gordon.

outside pack referee

noun

---

the referee position responsible for watching skaters on the outside of the track, focused on pack safety and actions.

CHAPTER 10:

Outside Looking In

Late Summer, 2010. Philadelphia, Pennsylvania.

"You lose a bet, Hymen?" a skater asks, snickering. I push tentatively forward on the borrowed white roller skates that are half-size too big for me. One moment of confidence is leading to another: I've decided I'm finally ready to get on skates. As a referee.

"Hymen-*pressed*," quips Robin Drugstores. Chewing gum, she plants her hands on her hips. I get a whiff of her cigarette smoke perfume as I roll by. "Announcers don't usually graduate to referees; you're doing this backwards." And she's not wrong. Typically, referees or skaters become announcers when they're done skating. Not the other way around.

"Shouldn't you retire or something, Drugs?" I say, shaking my head. Glancing at the referee whistle in my hand, I know I'm not ready to play this game, but I want to learn the rules better. Officiating seems like a good way to do that, if I can stay upright.

"I can't ever retire. They'll have to cut my skates off my feet," Drugs says.

"Cool, maybe they'll fit Hymen better than whatever the fuck she's wearing," Ivana Rock says, nodding her bleach-blonde hair towards me.

"I think your new name is, 'Hymen skates that are too big,'" Drugs says, then adds, "We're just teasing. We love you, Hymen."

"Five seconds," the jam timer, a non-skating official, calls from the inside of the track. Each roller derby game has three outside pack referees, an inside pack referee, a crew head referee, and two jammer referees—seven total on-skates refs. The newbs, like me, start on the outside—a hierarchy I quickly understand as skaters approach the track. Standing at the third turn of the track, I hear a whistle and watch the pack roll forward; a second whistle releases the jammers. Before I'm ready, the whole mess of skaters lurch towards me. I spring forward.

"Behind you," I hear another outside pack referee as he laps me on the right, keeping up with the pack that whisks past as I fall behind. Panic floods my brain. *I can't skate this fast.*

A double whistle sounds as the Butchers' jammer is called lead. But the Britches' jammer hits her out of bounds, forcing a call-off. I come to a shaky t-stop, dragging one skate on the floor behind me. The jam is over, and I'm already breaking a sweat. The crew head referee skates over to me from the inside of the track, whistle clenched in his teeth.

"You good?" he asks.

Still sucking for air, I nod. "I'm fine. My lungs, not so much."

"One piece of advice," he says with a wink. "Try to keep up."

I cough, nodding. I haven't been this out of breath since

giving birth; an equally painful learning process. As the next jam starts, I only hope I can keep up.

I wasn't the only one struggling to keep up with the explosive growth of roller derby. The WFTDA was fighting to clarify the rules and standards as fast as it could.

"The first rules of flat track roller derby were two pages," shares Amy Sherman, designer of the actual flat track. "A front and a back side of one piece of paper in 2002."

By the time 2010 rolled around, flat track's rules were forty-three pages[27]—including an appendix with Sherman's original track design. The diagram features measurements of the track, the outside referee lane, the penalty box, and the inside ref area. In flat track roller derby's twenty years, this track layout is one of the constants.

One major change, though, was the flow and pace of roller derby. Before 2009, speed was key in roller derby—a primary reason why I suspect the MavTV folks initially used NASCAR as their guide. The early days of the sport pulled inspiration from banked track, so the game started out fast. As teams like Oly began to practice more hockey-based techniques, like quick turns and stops, other teams followed suit and the game's flow naturally changed.

Bloody Mary's focus on insurance also started changing the game from a safety standpoint. The WFTDA decided to bring insurance in-house, to administer its own policy. Thus, penalties became more closely managed to keep injury claims to a minimum. The 2010 edition of *The Rules of Flat Track*

Roller Derby included well-described illegal actions like blocking to the back, blocking with the head, low blocks, and more.

Roller derby now had updated rules and new insurance. What I couldn't see at the time was how broadcast had wider implications for the development of all this. With clear, consistent broadcasts, skaters—like Oly Rollers—could watch games not just for fun, but to learn. So, too, could officials, coaches, and announcers. Thus, the better these broadcasts got, the more the community focused on what was important—the game itself.

Hymen's first referee patch.
Photo credit: Erica Vanstone.

recycling

verb

---

when a jammer is forced out of bounds and made to skate behind the pack.

CHAPTER 11:

My Kind of Town

November, 2010. Chicago, Illinois.

"Who let all these people into my room?" Riffing off a line from Frank Sinatra, I exhale these words into a microphone, speaking to more than five thousand screaming fans at the University of Illinois Chicago Pavilion for the 2010 WFTDA Championships. There's a power here, flickering from the back of my throat, into a piece of electronics and out into the roller derby universe.

As I look out over the blue and gray track, Windy City's *Uproar on the Lakeshore* hosts the largest audience I have ever seen at a roller derby event. This influx of fans in the UIC Pavilion is partly due to the growth of the number of clubs and teams. A huge driver of this has been *Whip It*—and streaming broadcast.

I turn to Val Capone and Margaret Thrasher, Windy and Gotham's announcers, respectively. We're an all-woman announcing crew, still a rarity despite this being a women's sport. I'm here as Philly's announcer again, and also to help coordinate Windy's broadcast with *DNN*. Bloody Mary wants me to figure out how financially and logistically feasible it would be for the WFTDA to run all this.

"But back to the action," I say. "Thrasher, who's on the jammer line?" Thrasher is a Gotham skater and New York actress who will later appear in television shows like *Happy* and *The Gilded Age*. For now, she's my buddy on the mic, leading this call with Val, a tall, dimpled Windy skater and announcer. Today I'm just the crowd wrangler.

"Mo Pain on the jammer line for Philly," she says. On the track in front of us, Philly Roller Girls take on Oly Rollers. Oly's skating style is changing the speed of the game. Instead of just skating faster, everyone alternates speed, makes quick changes, and even skates backwards. Oly and Rocky Mountain have both figured out how to do this with ease.

I feel a tug on my sleeve.

"D'you hear? *ESPN* might be here today," Val says off mic, pushing her face close to mine. I feel a rush of hot blood against my ear.

"*ESPN*," I can only echo. Taking in the UIC Pavilion, it occurs to me that interest from *ESPN* is another shift—an important one for roller derby. I feel a well of excitement and something else bubbling up: fear. I'm afraid of having an outsider come into our space—into *our room*. I don't want an outsider to miss the point. Again. Like MavTV.

I'm feeling protective. Motherly, even. My own son is with his father for the weekend, my now-estranged-husband. Like a lot of folks in roller derby, I'm feeling a sharp push-pull between roller derby life and my so-called *real life*.

I look over the sponsor reads to see if I've missed anything.

I don't have a blueprint here, or a map. I'm just going with the flow of the sport, following the energy. In my mind, my marriage is fair collateral damage to finding this kind of purpose. I'm not seeing the flaws in this logic yet. I only see opportunities for newness everywhere I look.

As it turns out, I wasn't the only one whose relationship had run aground because of roller derby. So many friends and colleagues have similar stories about exes, partners, or lovers.

"I would never have been allowed to play roller derby if I was still married," says The Cycrone, a.k.a. Jocelyn Jenik, former skater and general manager of then-Philly Roller Girls, now Philly Roller Derby. "My ex-husband would not have supported that in any way."

One of the most challenging truths behind roller derby's development is the stories like Jocelyn's and mine: stories of women finding themselves in roller derby, and the impact that has on significant relationships.

"Roller derby became my priority," Jenik shares. "[It] became my relationship."

Former WFTDA Executive Director Juliana Gonzales shares a similar experience.

"It was my work, it was my social spirit, it was my community, it was my everything." Many of us, me included, didn't necessarily see how much space roller derby was taking up because the validation was intoxicating. And as a result, we fiercely protected it. This protectiveness translated into the way we cultivated our work. In particular, the increasing fervor with which I was starting to develop my ideas around broadcast."

Now a dear friend, back when Bloody Mary and I had first been talking about my ideas to have WFTDA produce its own broadcast, she stopped me mid-conversation to say, "I think you need to want this a little less, Hymen."

These days, we laugh about it. But at the time, this was the first time anyone had called out—and with kindness—that I was deep in the thick of my own ego. That the intensity and drive I put into building the sport was palpable. And not always in a positive way.

"We understand better than anybody how to explain roller derby to people who have never seen [it] before," I told journalist Karen Hogan Ketchum in a 2012 interview for trade magazine *Sports Video Group*.[28] By the time she interviewed me about my approach to building our broadcasts, this excitement had become a near-obsession. A stay-at-home mom and an unfulfilled production coordinator, I saw the chance for something unprecedented and creative and heart-stopping. I love my son and wouldn't have changed a thing about being his mother. Yet, I also felt a void that led me to seek the validation and positive feedback that roller derby was giving me.

Motherhood was teaching me how to hold space; roller derby was teaching me how to take it. And amidst it all, I let my marriage fall to the wayside.

For better or for worse, establishing WFTDA broadcast was the key to unlocking the sport across a number of avenues—officiating, rules, marketing, and creative property ownership. Roller derby photographers became increasingly involved and built entire portfolios around showcasing the hits, the jumps, the laughter. And I became focused on cracking the code for how to bring all of it to the screen.

As a film school grad, I had the basics of filmmaking drilled into my head, semester after semester. The thing that stuck in my craw with roller derby broadcasts was the 180 degree rule. This is the basic tenet that says if you want to keep the audience oriented to the action, you need to keep them on the same side of that action—an imaginary line.

I was convinced there had to be a model with the right camera setup, high level announcing, great games—and that we could bring in money to keep it going. And I knew I wasn't the only one who felt this way.

Illustration by Sandra Frame,
a.k.a. Tara Arrnov.

stealing points

verb

---

when the lead jammer is too slow in calling off the jam to prevent her opponent from scoring points, the non-lead jammer is said to have stolen points.

CHAPTER 12:

The Commissioner

January, 2011. Philadelphia, Pennsylvania.

Jerry Seltzer calls himself *The Commissioner of Roller Derby*. As I step into a drafty warehouse in North Philadelphia on a January morning, I don't think he looks like the commissioner of anything other than sweatpants.

I spot him yards away with his back turned, standing at the base of a weathered roller derby banked track. Neon lights hang over him, illuminating the track. I've never met him before, but I've seen him enough on social media to know it's him.

Balding and in his seventies, he looks innocuous enough to me. Son of Leo Seltzer, who developed the original concept for roller derby in the 1920s, Jerry stands with both hands thrust into his sweat pockets. Before I can approach, a gruff voice and a cloud of cigarette smoke push towards me. I haven't smoked in over six years but the smell of tobacco is still enticing.

"Erica? That you?" Says the voice of a woman approaching from a makeshift office.

"Judy?" I ask, spotting the woman I've exchanged emails with, a stocky, auburn-haired woman spinning a whistle on a chain around her neck. Judy Sowinski, *The Polish Ace*, steps into dusty pools of light from the massive warehouse windows.

"Great to meet ya," Judy says, planting the remains of her cigarette into a nearby ashtray. Sowinski offers me a hug that resolves in a hearty slap on the back. She's what my parents' generation calls *the salt of the earth*. Right away, I like her.

Sowinski skated with banked track teams like the Philadelphia Warriors and Los Angeles Thunderbirds in the sixties and seventies. A coach now, her pedigree is more impressive to me than Seltzer's, but I don't say that aloud. Like most people in the community, I respect skaters more than promoters. I fall somewhere between the two and I know it.

I'm here because Seltzer sent an email to Philly, asking if anyone wanted to meet with him. As volunteer leadership now for both Philly Roller Girls and the WFTDA, I'm curious to hear what he has to say. Sowinski ushers me in, gesturing to the warehouse.

"A little drafty," she says. "Getting this place zoned for audiences is a bitch."

I nod, noting the lack of heating ducts and absence of visible bathrooms. Unlike in the heyday of banked track, when the Warriors played in West Philly, this frigid warehouse sits deep in the heart of North Philadelphia, an area that's been decimated by a century of redlining. Neighborhoods have been getting gentrified around the country, making them harder to afford.

Penn Jersey's warehouse is full of skaters, and it's a similar demographic to Philly Roller Girls, who practice in Camden. Like Penn Jersey, Philly Roller Girls is also mostly white, middle class. I catch the designer label on the Commissioner's sweatsuit as I draw near.

I was told Seltzer is touring the dozen or so banked track clubs to see if there's a possibility to get a more formal circuit going. Selfishly, I wonder if he has connections to *ESPN*. Or any broadcast funding, for that matter. Sowinski introduces me.

"You ever try banked track?" Seltzer asks, nodding to it.

"No," I say. "I'm a referee, though."

"I like banked track better—but I'm biased," Sowinski says. I respect her candor.

"Banked track and flat track need to work together," Seltzer says. "There's no reason we can't all benefit from cross-promotion. Just look at *Whip It*."

Announcers across the country tell me Seltzer's been having these conversations with lots of flat track clubs. His involvement with television spectacles like *RollerJam* in the late 1990s is how he got his moniker *The Commissioner*. For *RollerJam*, he created a fictional World Skating League and added scripted fights and beefs. This has led to skepticism from the WFTDA.

We don't want him adding any alligator pits to roller derby is a common refrain among leadership. Watching the skaters on the banked track fall and bounce back up, I'm impressed. Using flexibility from the wood, the momentum and the physics of the track to propel themselves forward, the skaters look joyful. I can see the appeal.

"Flat track is changing," Seltzer says as we sit on bleachers nearby. "The WFTDA rule set is getting slower. It sucks for fans. Roller derby was designed for speed, to go faster."

"'S'more fun that way," Sowinski adds.

Sowinski, a former skater, I trust. The Commish, not so much.

"With all due respect, this is the version of the sport they—" but I stop myself. I'm part of this now. Not just a bystander. "The version of the sport *we* want to play."

Seltzer shakes his head. "Fans are confused. And bored. If you can't build a fanbase, you don't have a sport. You have a really badass-looking Girl Scout troop."

His sentiment —a quick nod to *Whip It*'s "Hurl Scouts"— causes my fists to clench.

"Okay, but we're the ones with the cookies everyone wants to eat," I say, causing him to grin. I can tell he's not going to give up on this easily. "Sorry, I just don't believe that banked track has the foothold on the community right now that flat track does. Besides, banked tracks are expensive," I add. This causes Seltzer to chuckle, and I realize exactly who I'm saying this to, the man who booked roller derby to sold-out crowds at arenas in the sixties and seventies. He laughs at me, and I clear my throat.

"Let me ask you a question," he says. And I know when a man prefaces a question with a statement like this, it's usually not a good question. "Flat track doesn't really have staying power, does it? The game is getting almost unwatchable." An indictment more than a question.

"If you call over four thousand people at the UIC Pavilion in Chicago unwatchable."

"What if it could be five thousand?" Seltzer asks. "Ten thousand? These are the numbers I used to pull in back in the day." That he uses an *I* statement clues me in that he doesn't view roller derby as a collaborative effort, but a product. *His product.* "What about a joint event, to start?" He adds. *There it is. He wants us to help promote him.*

I shake my head. "It would just confuse fans."

"It would sell tickets," Seltzer says.

"We're volunteer-run. Our overhead is a lot lower."

"Cutting costs isn't growth."

He wasn't wrong. But I wasn't there to debate our value. "We're growing enough that we just added London Rollergirls," I say, shrugging. "Europe, Canada."

"Great, that's what we want." Again, he inserts himself into modern roller derby. I'm sure he doesn't think I notice. "But how will you really capitalize on the growth without money?"

Broadcast. I know the answer but I don't say it out loud. I don't want him to know I'm about to launch a roller derby channel on the internet, lest he try to insert himself in that, too. And it's clear that he needs us more than we need him. That we own the assets, the value.

"We'll figure it out," I say. And I decide right then and there that I don't want this man's money, his promotion, or his contacts. Roller derby will do what we've always done: *We'll figure it out. Our way.*

hockey stop

noun

---

using the edges of your skate
wheels to carve a sharp curve that
stops forward momentum.

CHAPTER 13:

Pay Per View

Spring, 2011. Philadelphia, Pennsylvania.

"People don't want to pay to watch roller derby." I'm replaying the words in my head uttered by a member of the WFTDA Board of Directors as I look at the fifteen hundred or so fans watching us in the Class of 1923 Arena. We're in the University of Pennsylvania's aging hockey arena. This game is Philly's first foray into a bigger venue, and it sure as hell looks like folks are willing to pay to watch us.

I'm in a short black skirt, wearing an officials' shirt, or what we call *zebra stripes*. Instead of announcing, I'm officiating. The word *Heaven* and the number *29* adorns the back of my shirt in a small black patch the Cycrone made me. I watch the pack of Philthy Britches and Broad Street Butchers work its way past the jammer line, around turns one and two, and over towards me—the outside pack referee stationed at turn four.

The Butchers and Britches battle it out on our bright blue and gray sport court for the Warrior Cup, the top prize for Philly's home teams. As skaters approach, I pick up speed to meet them. Antidote, the Butchers jammer, sprints through the pack and the crowd roars. It's a deafening sound that spurs me on.

"Five point pass for Antidote and the Broad Street Butchers," Eddie Spaghetti proclaims, now alone on the mic as I keep up with the pack in my too-big skates. My eyes are on the action, on trying to referee this game, but my head is stuck in this broadcast conversation. On the value of roller derby.

A streaming company out of Portland produced the Sacramento playoff last year. They use DVD sales and pay-per-view to afford their broadcasts. I told the Board we can do this, too.

We're not trying to get rich, I'd said. *We just want to cover costs.*

On the track in front of me, the pack rolls to a stop as the red and white-clad Broad Street Butchers slow the blue wall of Britches behind them. Butcher Shenita Stretcher is in a two-wall with Mary that Motha Oh God. Antidote, her jammer, approaches the pack again behind Britches Gloria Grindem and Violet Temper, both in blue. Crouching low, Shenita lays a massive hit, only she's facing the wrong way, a clockwise block that's illegal. I blow my whistle.

"Red three-oh-five, clockwise block," I yell, waving my right hand back and forth, the clockwise block signal for Shenita to leave the track. She grins and shrugs at me, then heads to the penalty box as Antidote clears her scoring run. The crowd erupts, cheering on the Butchers' twenty-point jam. We've gone from a few hundred in a Camden roller rink to nearly two thousand people in a small arena.

I can feel it in my bones that we have the fanbase to support a broadcast program. That this community wants to see themselves. WFTDA Board isn't so sure; they feel pay-per-view is a barrier—especially for a community where everyone already pays to participate. Still, the WFTDA's new insurance program was charging skaters a small fee for annual insurance so there was precedent. It could work. And I'm not the only one who believes that.

Joe Christensen was a newly married IT professional when he made the decision to quit his desk job and form a video production company, Blaze Streaming Media. While I was obsessing over variables needed for roller derby to look good, Christensen was digging into the tools to bring it to life technically. I was a film school grad desperate to express the art of roller derby, Christensen was an engineer aching to get at the science of it. We both had what the other was looking for, especially since Christensen had purchased one critical piece of gear.

"This piece of equipment, the TriCaster, was a rebel," he says in a recent conversation. "It was like having a television studio on a computer." Introduced in 2005 by NewTek, a Texas production company, the TriCaster[29] was described as "a portable live production suite." After investing $12,000 of his life's savings into the piece of gear, Christensen floated around Portland, Oregon trying to find a good use for it. After *Northwest Knockdown*, he stumbled across Rose City Rollers.

"As the production company owner, I didn't accept any money from them," Christensen says, "but I needed to pay my crew, most of whom were Rose City volunteers. And $100 bucks a night plus roller derby and all of the free beer you could drink was a pretty good deal."

Roller derby, Christensen, and his TriCaster were in the right place at the right time. He had a willing laboratory for experimenting with on-site streaming. And I was looking for a vendor willing to let us retain creative ownership.

"Honestly, we put cameras in the wrong place at first," Christensen admits, describing his early experience with roller derby in a 2012 interview with Sports Video Group.[30] While Christensen was a businessman with a nose for technology, what he lacked at that point was experience in roller derby. Conversely, grassroots productions folks like Madison's Hinckley Productions and *Derby News Network* were producing community streams. A hindrance for them scaling was often internet quality and consistent camera operators.

Christensen offered stable, quality streams and service.

"I wasn't interested in shaping the story, I was interested in the mechanics of serving this audience, roller derby," Christensen says. He wanted to find ways to improve the process of roller derby broadcast, and I had a pretty good use for his findings.

Christansen made his services affordable, cost-wise, for the growing WFTDA. He used Rose City's volunteers, including a referee, Speedbump—a.k.a. Benjamin Doyle—whose basketball production background laid the groundwork for a new camera setup. Blaze offered the WFTDA a fifty/fifty split on cost and revenue. He put his own skin in the game, lessening the financial burden for a sport still learning to make money.

"I became enamored with the idea [a roller derby

channel] could be a self supporting product or service," says Christensen. "That it could generate revenue that flows back to the organization."

He and I both had sons the same age—only, I was a newly-single mother. We were both trying to build something meaningful in our lives, something of value. And not just in roller derby. Christensen was also an ally and champion of women's sports, and the first professional from outside of roller derby who validated my vision.

"The idea that I would be a part of a sport that was created and nurtured by women is perfect," he says. "The question of roller derby being taken seriously—I took it seriously. I devoted so much time and effort and passion to making this work, so I took it seriously."

Taking our ideas seriously was the key to making progress. Heading into 2011, I succeeded in brokering a deal with the WFTDA and Blaze to produce events, including the upcoming 2011 Championships. We weren't asking if roller derby was worth paying for, we were proving it already was.

rink rash

noun

---

during a fall, when a skater's
naked skin slides across the track,
causing an abrasion that leaves
red welts.

CHAPTER 14:

Paradigm Shift

June, 2011. Feasterville, Pennsylvania.

Why are we making it harder for women to be women?
Isn't biology enough to determine gender?
I don't want to skate with men, this is the WFTDA. The "W" is
for "Women's!"

It's eight o'clock on a June morning and I'm standing on
the mezzanine at the Sportsplex in Feasterville. With dark,
curly hair and glasses, Kim Deal With It towers over me. Kim,
a transgender woman, sports a long, black skirt and striped
rainbow socks. She reads through social media and shares
Philly's very public response to the WFTDA's latest gender
policy discussion, and it's contentious: Should hormones
define womanhood?

Philly's open letter says, *"We believe that using hormone levels*
to define 'female' is a slippery slope that leads to discrimination
against all skaters..." This discussion echoes conversations
Philly reps have had in WFTDA forums and was co-written
by league leadership, and one of our referees, also a transgender woman. This is the first public dissent from a WFTDA

team. And it won't be the last.

Kim looks up at me. I don't know her non-derby name. What I would refer to as a *government name*, she refers to as a *dead name*, the name of a person she no longer inhabits. Since Philly's open letter was shared on social media this week, comments across platforms like Twitter and Facebook have been frenzied and divided.

I glance at my son sitting on a faded brown couch nearby, coloring. This is my weekend for custody, so I'm taking him to work—derby work. He takes a bite of donut with his stuffed animal, Lamby, in the crook of his arm. Secretly, I hope being around conversations like this can help him build empathy. After a pause, Kim says, "Still doesn't address what to do with nonbinary skaters, but it's a start."

"Are we allowed to discuss it on the mic?" an announcer asks, pushing his square glasses back up the bridge of his nose. "On our game calls?"

"Yes, but this is a skater policy, so we should tread lightly." I'm seeing the cracks in the foundation of everything we're building. I'd rather not widen those cracks. Everyone nods and disperses for our first games of the day.

I follow two announcers over to the side of the mezzanine where they prep for their broadcast call. A set of headphones sits on a broken wooden table overlooking the second track, featuring a game that's about to take place between Gotham and Madison. Folding my arms, I squint out at the track.

"Geez, no pressure, Double H," another announcer says, taking a seat.

"Huh?" I ask. "What did you say?"

"You're hovering over us, like George Orwell," he says. "No pressure or anything."

"No, I got that. What's *Double H?*"

"It's you," he says. "Hymen Heaven. Two 'H's. Like Triple H, the wrestler."

"Double H." I echo. Admittedly, the name has a certain ring to it.

With all this talk of gender policy and identities, I hadn't realized that my own name, my own persona, had begun to feel constricted, and a little bit outdated. Perhaps no longer in service of who I am—or who I'm becoming. Although, I'm still not sure I know who that is. Just that everything's changing.

When the WFTDA designed its gender policy in 2010, it was among the most progressive in women's sports. Yet, it included "that the athlete's sex hormones are within the medically acceptable range for a female."[31] Even this iteration of the policy allowed teams to ask a skater for medical documentation, opening the door for discrimination.

"The problem with sports is that they can be a great engine for social change but in the end, someone has to win and someone has to lose," Stefanie Madison, the announcer formerly known as Kim Deal With It, shares with me in a recent chat. Women were often on the losing end; trans women even more so.

Most gender policies attached to governing bodies shared this bias, like the International Olympic Committee and its roller derby pathway, the Federation of International Roller Sports—now, World Skate.[32] These federations chose hormone levels to define womanhood. For example, a 2024 *Newsweek article* about the 2024 Olympic policies around transgender athletes, stating that the rules were "intended to prevent any perceived unfair advantages."[33]

This idea of *fairness* was baked into Title IX[34] from the beginning: that certain hormones equate to cheating. Even the WFTDA's early policy required a *medically acceptable* hormone level from a person's medical care team. Essentially, a doctor's note.

Yet, as the sport of roller derby itself changed, the needs of its athletes changed with it. Some of those needs included space and equity for transgender women, and shifting ideas about how the sport was physically played. Alongside a constant cry for body positivity, different shapes and sizes were not only welcome but needed in roller derby. The Olympic or NCAA assertion that women were frail objects needing to be *protected* simply didn't hold in a contact sport on roller skates.

For the first time, the "W" in "WFTDA" didn't just stand for *women*, in my mind. It stood for *"who"* and *"what"* we were willing to stand for. I saw broadcast as a way to reflect that truth. I hadn't expected it to be reflected back to me by my own son.

It's early fall 2011 and my son's eyes are wide like half-moons. He's peering over the steel counter at Lorenzo's on South Street. It's our regular lunch date; a single mom's attempt to get her son to behave at preschool. If he stops using his fists to resolve conflict, every Friday I pick him up and take him to lunch. Usually pizza.

The clerk behind the counter nods at my Philly Roller Girls shirt. "Roller derby?" He asks, taking my money.

"Yup," I say, pulling stools next to the metal counter on the other side of the shop.

The clerk pretends to elbow imaginary people, asking, "Like wrestling?"

I laugh. "Not exactly." The clerk smiles and hands us our slices. I turn away from him and toward my kid. "You still having issues with any boys in school?" I ask, watching him bite into his gooey slice.

"Just one kid. He took Lamby," he says, nodding to Lamby, a graying stuffed animal who sits on the counter watching us eat pizza.

"But you walked away, right? That's what we talked about?"

"Yeah." He takes tiny nibbles out of a round piece of pepperoni.

I tear a morsel of crust and offer it to Lamby. "Is Lamby hungry?"

"No," he says, quickly, definitively. "She had French toast sticks for breakfast."

"That explains the maple syrup on his face."

"Mom, Lamby's not a *he*," my son adds. "Lamby's a girl." He shrugs.

I switch it up. "Well, if she gets hungry, let me know." Gender, I now understand, is more than a label. A truth roller derby taught me. My son nods, taking the sippy cup I brought from his lunch box. For the first time, I'm feeling what's truly at stake with all of this work I'm doing: building not just a sport on empathy, but a community. My son and I have never talked about gender, but he's clearly listened. Suddenly, I can't help but wonder: What legacy will this sport leave for his generation, now that we're ten years in?

Taking a nap while mom builds broadcast.
Photo credit: Erica Vanstone.

partner
blocking

noun

---

when two blockers work together
to hold back a jammer.

CHAPTER 15:

Continental Divide

September, 2011. Indianapolis, Indiana.

"Welcome back to the 2011 WFTDA Championships, live from Broomfield, Colorado. I'm Double H and I am joined here by Hydra."

Mic in hand, I stand next to Hydra, the woman after whom the WFTDA's trophy is named. She's a few inches shorter, with cropped, straight blond hair and a black and white-striped shirt. I'm nervous; the lights are bright and I'm trying to keep my cool.

"We often refer to Texas Rollergirls as the godmothers of flat track roller derby," I say to her. "And you are one of those godmothers." Hydra's a legend, and I feel I'm standing on hallowed ground. Both of our microphones have flags that say *WFTDA* on them—a nice touch that Blaze Streaming Media included for our broadcasts.

This year, Gotham is on a roll led by Bonnie Thunders and Suzy Hotrod, jammers who helped beat last year's Champions, Rocky Mountain, by fifty points. A handful of strategies have taken hold this weekend that skaters will no doubt want to rewatch. Our wins feel collective.

"I'm really impressed with the level of play," Hydra says, turning to the track behind us and talks about the early days in Austin. "Back then, hardly anybody knew about roller derby, and we were just trying to get the sport known to the public."

I look up to see the camera operator nodding. He catches my eye and gives me a thumbs up. I can't help but smile. All of the elements are coming together: games, camera work, interviews, announcing. We're on pay-per-view, with a free low quality option, just as I'd pitched the Board. And...people were loving it. We'd brought in over $100,000 this fall—every dollar reinvested in production. Even Hydra notices.

"What's your hope for the future?" I ask her.

"I'd hate to see the skaters, for any control to slip out of their hands. And I think we're on the right track—international play, just to continue on the path to world domination."

"World domination." I echo this as a battle cry. With broadcast, I have a very specific idea for how we could reach this milestone. As it turns out, sports media was catching on, too.

But was everyone tuning in for the right reasons? Jane McManus nails it in an October 2011[35] article previewing Gotham Girls Roller Derby jammer Suzy Hotrod's appearance in *ESPN: The Magazine*. "Most people will see Suzy Hotrod naked before they see her play roller derby."

And they did. Suzy Hotrod is, in fact, naked in the 2011 *ESPN Bodies We Want*[36] issue. Roller derby's inclusion in *Bodies We Want* was huge. Unlike *Sports Illustrated's* famous swimsuit issue, which traditionally featured scantily clad models, *ESPN*'s version used nudity to showcase athletics. Conversely, *Sports Illustrated* perpetuated a different reality, one dependent on the male gaze to drive sales.

"The *Swimsuit Issue* sold something like ten times as much as any other issue," says *The Athletic*'s Emma Span, a former *Sports Illustrated* staffer. "It was a massive moneymaker for them—income when subscriptions were down and web ads weren't paying."

At least *ESPN* tried to do something different with naked athletes. In her reporting, McManus—herself a jammer with Suburbia Roller Girls in 2011—calls attention to the fact that, either way, sex sells, and in roller derby, it's been a key part of the sport.

Yet, placing Suzy Hotrod, a.k.a. New York photographer Jean Schwarzwalder, next to athletes like Hope Solo, Apolo Anton Ohno, and Jose Reyes pushed roller derby towards legitimacy. A legitimacy I was eager to claim, partly as a push-back to Jerry Seltzer's idea of the sport, partly to move the needle forward on getting our own broadcast deals.

"We have to dispel preconceived notions about theatrics and goofy wrestling antics, so we train really hard," Hotrod shares with *ESPN*'s *Bodies We Want*.[37] Indeed, how the media covered us was increasingly important.

"Oftentimes, newspapers or media will know what they're gonna cover," says McManus, a journalist and skater herself. "It's [dictated from the] top down—we're gonna cover the Flyers, the 76ers. Those things get covered really well. Then it's up to us [writers] to say hey, 'I got this idea off of the beat, here's the pitch.' Pre-pandemic, that would mean a whole lot of things are covered as one offs—and that's how roller derby gets covered."

One-off pieces, however, didn't hamper roller derby's growth. By 2012, the organization would reach more than 171 clubs; a 511% increase since its inception in 2005. Legitimate sport or no, roller derby was exploding. Yes, it was punk rock, and yes, it was athletic—and yes, it was sexy. It was simultaneously all of these things. As a result, no one in the media fully knew what to do with us. But I did.

Continental Divide and Conquer, 2010.
Photo credit: Erica Vanstone.

watch party

noun

---

gathering friends to watch a
streamed roller derby game
at home.

CHAPTER 16:

The Enemy of Success

Fall, 2012. Fort Wayne, Indiana.

The good news? We launched our new website this fall for broadcast, WFTDA.tv. The bad news? The website has crashed. I'm at the 2012 WFTDA Playoffs in Fort Wayne, Indiana, watching the Tweets roll in.

My stream is down!

Refund, WFTDA.tv! #Talk2WFTDA

#Talk2WFTDA This is why free is better

Instead of celebrating our site and fancy new graphics, I'm sitting trackside in a convention center staring at an error screen. Refreshing my laptop several times doesn't help. Checking my inbox, I see frustrated emails flooding in about the problem, causing people to miss a handful of exciting playoff games. And it's all my responsibility.

Hopping on the phone with our web host, our volunteer tech team and I learn that the website broke because of high demand. This year, on WFTDA.tv, we made the whole postseason pay-per-view. And the demand caused the monetization app to fail. The plug-in collecting money from viewers was never designed for this kind of heavy lifting, and it melted the website. I console myself with the notion that this type of failure is a good kind of failure, brought on by a successful broadcast. *There's data in failure.*

"What's your solution?" Bloody Mary asks me on the phone as she watches the online panic from several states away, in Texas. Never one to beat around the bush, Bloody demonstrates that when mistakes happen, hand wringing is irrelevant.

"We gotta take everything out from behind the paywall," I say, echoing my conversations with Joe Christensen at Blaze Streaming Media. "Let folks see the games and we'll sort the money out later." Maybe we lose money this week but have everything back up and running next week. Maybe we fall on our faces and fuel the community's anger around charging money to watch roller derby to begin with. Or maybe it's just one hiccup in a long line of future successes that'll feel like the distant past in a few months.

"Do it," Bloody says. "The community being able to watch is the most important thing."

Sitting back down at the dais, I see Twitter is all over this.

Make broadcast free! #Talk2WFTDA

Stop being so greedy, WFTDA.

People have every right to be upset. To me, this isn't about greed, it's about paying for services that put resources back into the sport we love. And I'm not even getting paid for this job right now. Just then, I see a text flashing from my ex-husband.

Can you talk to your son? He misses you. A deeper pang hits my gut; a reminder of more failure as a whole community sharpens its pitchforks. I decide the person who needs me the most is the one not in the room right now and step outside to call my kid.

A week after WFTDA.tv went down, *Derby News Network* published an Op-Ed, railing against pay-per-view broadcasts: "Pay Per View is the Enemy of Success."

"This year, for the first time ever, the live online broadcasts of roller derby's top competitive events are viewable only for people who are willing to pay to watch. Many (many) people in the derby community have expressed dissatisfaction with this course of action. We agree; we think it's very shortsighted and counterproductive to place obstacles between the sport and its potential audience."

DNN's own broadcast model relied heavily on a donations-based system, and most of their budget was coming directly out of the founders' pockets. In fairness, they had their own business to protect. And they had spearheaded much of community streaming.

Internally, our own WFTDA volunteers worked their butts off to pull this together with me; Deadeye, a soft spoken non-binary coding whiz from San Francisco had built WFTDA.tv *with their own hands*. Unpaid marketing volunteers like Lois Slain, Tamarra Neverdyes, and so many others worked on public Tweets and responses. Baam Baam from Madison, Kim Deal With It, and other announcers began crafting clearer standards for calls. All of this showed in the production quality… when the website was working.

My friend Tank, Ohio's announcer-turned-blogger with followers in his own right, penned a rebuttal to *DNN* in his blog, *Roller Derby Inside Track*.[38]

He argued that, "UFC and WWE pay per views cost $55 for 2.5-3 hours' worth of action. $55 for 3 hours [from UFC] vs. $50 for 15 DAYS [from the WFTDA]." His point? Compared to other sports, roller derby was still cheap.

It also wasn't lost on WFTDA leadership that quite a bit of community media was being spearheaded by men—including *Derby News Network*, Tank's own *Roller Derby Inside Track*, and podcast *Derby Deeds*. And later WindyMan's *Roller Derby Notes* and *The Apex*. All of these sites were men championing women.

"When I started, it was absolutely the community that drove me," Jason "Megatron" Burrows tells me. "I poured so much of my mental and work energy into this podcast—I didn't do my day job for years."

Burrows launched the *Deeds* podcast in 2010. Like most of the founders of *Derby News Network*, Megatron was a man carving a role for himself in a feminist women's sport. At times, the push and pull of this became exhausting on both sides. WFTDA.tv soon became a place where the mother organization drew a line in the sand. One that said, *this belongs to us.* And not everyone liked that.

Yet, as you know, roller derby has never given a fuck about who likes us or not.

Weeks later, I'm producing a game at the 2012 WFTDA

Championships in Atlanta. And I'm battling more than a few problems. WFTDA.tv is back up and running, but the tournament organizers weren't able to get our cameras high enough. The coverage looks flat, compressed.

Next, all of the teams at Championships have started picking up each other's strategies by watching our streams. Games are less predictable, more suspenseful—but they're also slower.

But what's taking my full attention right now is that my play-by-play broadcaster for this call, Koolaid, sounds like he's been gargling glass shards.

"Three on three in the pack," Koolaid says, clearing his throat. Usually smooth, knowledgeable, relaxed, right now he sounds strained and gravely, like he's been screaming on the sidelines for his team, the Texecutioners. And it hurts me to listen. I write a note and pass it to him. *You sound like shit, talk quieter.*

He nods and writes a note in return. *Water?* I reach for a fresh bottle nearby and open it, then hand it to him. *Thank you,* he mouths.

"We had that conversation with Tannibal Lector earlier," his announcing partner Baam Baam, jumps in. "She's got that hernia brace on to support the muscle girdle." That Lector is even skating at all is either incredible or unconscionable, depending on who you ask. Yet, it doesn't seem to slow Oly down as they try to battle to take back the Hydra from Gotham.

Wow, Gotham is crushing Oly! #Talk2WFTDA

#Talk2WFTDA These replays are sick!

Yay for moms in roller derby! We love Oly!

Reading these Tweets, I suddenly realize: people aren't

complaining about the feed, or the quality right now. They're just excited about the game.

All any sport could ever hope for is that the production speaks for itself, for the work to be so proficient, that nobody's noticing the elements. That, to me, is what a great sports broadcast is all about. Here in Atlanta, I see glimmers of it coming together. Glimmers, I hope, of how a handful of women with filthy names and fishnets built something that's about to take on the wide world of sports.

Only, instead of feeling satisfied that we just overcame the implosion of our entire digital broadcast enterprise, I'm feeling the opposite—hungry to learn more. Eager to make broadcast better and better. Even if it meant exploring unlikely avenues for inspiration.

Bloody Mary and Catman, 2013.
Photo credit: Erica Vanstone.

natural grand slam

noun

---

when a jammer scores all five possible five points, as in baseball, while the opposing jammer is still on the track.

CHAPTER 17:

Let's Play Ball

February, 2013. Camden, New Jersey.

A few months after WFTDA.tv's first season, I'm back to exploring more ideas; this time by getting inspiration from minor league baseball.

"You announce baseball before?" The creative services director for the Camden Riversharks walks me through the bowels of Campbell's Field, a small stadium on the banks of the Delaware River across from Philadelphia. The place smells of grass and fertilizer, years-old fry grease, and stale beer. These are smells I find enticing—the scent of sports. Even in roller derby, we have these types of sensory guides, notes to let us know we're in the right place.

"I've announced roller derby for five years," I say, then add, "I played softball for five years, too." Though my softball experience was almost two generations ago, in fifth grade. Not that I tell her that.

"I played softball too," she says in a tone I interpret as sympathetic. "Let's try you out on the mic." She shoots me a knowing glance. I've never met another woman announcing for baseball. Her look tells me maybe she hasn't either. I've been an announcer, a referee, a broadcaster for the sport of roller derby. But I wanted to understand how we compared to other sports; to know if there was a secret sauce we were missing in production. So when the Riversharks' ad for public address announcers popped up, I sent my resume right over.

The director opens the door to the press box, a room with a row of gray counters and electrical outlets. A giant metal gate covers what I assume is the window bay looking out onto the field. She takes a key from the lanyard and unlocks the side, then pushes it upward. The late-winter baseball diamond reveals itself.

Campbell's Field joins the base of the Benjamin Franklin Bridge, overlooking the city of Philadelphia. Its stoic marble is an impressive back wall to the field. A white tarp covers the dirt of the diamond, but a groundskeeper below meticulously inspects the muddy grass. It all feels open, welcoming. Fresh. *I wish my son was here to see this.* I can picture him in his red Phillies hoodie, eating ice cream in rows of seats like the ones in front of me.

"Wow," I whisper without meaning to. The stadium feels religious, almost church-like.

"Beats working in an office," she says. Now, I understand why she'd want to blend in with the other khaki-clad men on this minor league baseball team. It's a space that women aren't often invited into—a space in the church where we're not allowed to pray.

She picks up a black and silver microphone resting against the soundboard. Turning on the switch underneath it, a squeak echoes from the ballpark speakers. Tapping her fingers against the edge of the mic, she lifts it to her lips and speaks.

"Check one, check two," she says, and her voice returns to us.

A question occurs to me. "Am I the first woman you guys have interviewed?"

"No," she says, adjusting the sound board's knobs. "But you'd be the first one we've hired if you get the job." She hands me the microphone, then the small stack of papers with the reads on them. I glance at the list of names.

"Read these," she says.

I take a deep breath, pushing out into my diaphragm and relaxing my shoulders. Lowering my voice, I speak with my full chest into the microphone, "Ladies and gentlemen, welcome to Campbell's Field. Now batting for the Riversharks, third baseman Paddy Matera..."

Something about the echo of my voice across Campbell's Field, bouncing off the base of the Ben Franklin Bridge in the hot summer air, is utterly perfect. Not because this was the big leagues, but the opposite. It has *proximity*. You can touch everything—smell it, taste it. A physicality that invites you in.

When I first joined the Camden Riversharks in 2013, I was the only woman announcer they had, and the first woman they eventually let on a broadcast. Though the job paid roughly $20 a game, the money wasn't as important to me as the experience. I wanted to learn as much as I could from other sports, especially when it came to announcing and broadcasting.

Minor league baseball, like roller derby, didn't have a lot of money to throw at bells and whistles. Their broadcasts were audio-only, and they also had a table with its stats keepers. I'd watch over their shoulders as they used software called Pointstreak[39] to collect data from the game. As I did, I was able to validate what roller derby broadcast was doing with our graphics and score overlay, and it gave me the idea to also lean into audio broadcasts.

For example, their rain delay tarp had a sponsor's logo on it. This helped spark conversations around putting floor stickers on our tracks to sell as a sponsorship which would not only be seen by in-venue fans, but also on WFTDA.tv broadcasts.

Yet, unaffiliated baseball and roller derby struggled with some common problems—one that eventually led the Riversharks to disband—which was the ability to bring in consistent revenue. Whether a nonprofit or for-profit revenue model, all smaller sports struggle to bring in money.

I didn't necessarily understand where broadcast's revenue fell into the equation, budget-wise, for the WFTDA. I knew that we'd brought in almost $150,000 in 2012, despite the website crashing. It wasn't much, in broader sports terms but it was enough to cover the cost of our fledgling enterprise. Out of this, the WFTDA Board and Bloody Mary had decided this revenue was too important not to have a paid job attached to it. The Director of Broadcast Operations position was created, and I applied.

This growth signaled WFTDA broadcast's moderate success. At least, enough to pique the curiosity of certain folks with a vested interest. Folks like Jerry Seltzer.

hit it and quit it

verb

---

when a jammer grabs as many points as she can in a scoring pass before calling off the jam, usually to prevent an opponent from scoring points.

CHAPTER 18:

Rules of Engagement

September, 2013. Oakland, California.

"What do you mean, I can't get in?"

It's fall 2013 and Jerry Seltzer stands at the door of the West Region Playoffs venue—a warehouse on the bay in Oakland, California.

"You're welcome to come in," a volunteer says. "Just not for free. You can pay like everybody else." It's late afternoon and a San Francisco sunset pushes through on the west side of the venue, facing the water. Floor-height windows are framed by dramatic black velvet curtains—they line a concrete skating surface with a taped oval in the middle. And right now, these same curtains are keeping me hidden like a dance mom, peeking from backstage.

The sounds of live, modern roller derby surround me: whistles, cheers. Announcers hollering about points. My eyes are glued to Seltzer, who stands near the door of the venue, red-faced. I keep myself out of sight—I don't want him waving me over to help him. One of the ticketing volunteers from Bay Area Derby walks past.

"What's that about?" I ask, nodding Jerry's direction. I adjust a name tag on my blazer that reads *Double H, WFTDA Director of Broadcast Operations*. My new full-time job. After going through a rigorous interview process, I was relieved to get hired in an actual job in roller derby—something that's still quite rare. Yet now that I'm *WFTDA-official*, I don't want to gain Seltzer's attention.

"He wants to know why his name's not on the list," she says.

"The list?" I poke my head out further to watch him.

"Of comped entries." She flips her long, blue hair and walks away. From a distance, I watch the standoff. The Board member folds her arms, cocking her dyed-blonde hair to the side as Seltzer throws up his hands and walks away. She stands there for a moment as he turns to go.

I've never seen a woman stand her ground like this before, like a bouncer at a club. Probably not what the Commissioner of roller derby was expecting. I'm in awe. He shuffles off, waving at a skater or two as he goes, opting to step outside. Always cheerful, always a networker. I'm not sure if he'll return, but the Board member walks in my direction.

"Told him he's not on the list," she says, meeting my eyes as she approaches. "Thinks he has dominion over roller derby. He can pay just like everyone else."

"For real," I say, straightening. Instead of being a colleague, this Board member is now technically my boss. I'm not sure if I should act differently, but I smile awkwardly and nod until she walks away. Then, I exhale.

A tall brunette skater from Angel City skates by.

"Double H, do you have any tape?"

"Tape?" I blink.

"For my elbow pad, it keeps falling off." She shows me a Velcro strap to the side of her pad that keeps falling. Most skaters use tape to keep worn gear in place—sometimes past its use. Then, she adds, "Oh, I forget, you're not a skater."

As she skates away towards the bleachers, her words sting a bit. It's true, I'm not a skater. I've put all of this time and energy into something I've never even tried. And I'm starting to understand a truth I haven't quite vocalized: By the skater, for the skater is very intentionally not "by the officials, for the officials." Or "by announcers, for announcers."

Almost everything in roller derby is run by skater consensus. With both positive and negative results. But were skaters always the best-equipped to make those decisions? I was learning to navigate this question. Even as another idea was starting to take shape: what would happen if I just became a skater?

In 2013, roller derby was at a tipping point. Recent rules changes included the double-whistle jam start being eliminated, along with minor penalties. Changes like this were strategically brilliant. Yet, they slowed the game and fans didn't like that. Especially Jerry Seltzer.

"Slow derby started to hit leagues in the pocket books," says Rose City Executive Director, Kim Stegeman—a.k.a. Rocket Mean. "In the heyday of roller derby's growth, from 2010 on, we had so much emphasis on DIY that we didn't talk about running businesses."

The push and pull between what the athletes wanted and what potential fans might want became visible. Rule changes evolved out of how skaters wanted to play the game, not for how they would impact ticket sales. Minor league baseball, with all of its cheesiness, still packaged games with trivia, dollar hot dogs, and theme nights to please fans.

Because of this rift, bloggers like *Roller Derby Notes*[40] proclaimed 2013 to be the year that was "The End of the Beginning," the end of everyone being on the same page with where the sport should go. As for me? If I was going to peddle the *by the skater, for the skater* ethos, I wanted to at least try to become a skater. Not an official. Not an announcer. A *skater*. Just to see what all the fuss was about.

Illustration by Sandra Frame,
a.k.a. Tara Armov.

get lower

verb

---

a common directive in roller derby, reminding skaters to adjust their center of gravity so they can withstand hits more effectively.

CHAPTER 19:

A Sense of Urgency

November, 2013. Camden, New Jersey.

"Where's your sense of urgency!" Holden Killfield screams from across the roller rink. Leaning on the cinderblock wall, she watches a dozen of us skate around an oval track. We're back in Camden, only this time, I'm not a referee. I'm a skater—or, trying to be. I'm training to be a brand-new Philly Roller Girls skater, a member of *fresh meat.*

"Urgency," Kill says again. Grunting, I push my legs faster. "Much better, Double H."

I exhale. Skating on the track is different from skating on the outside of the track. Outside pack referees, at least, skate for about half the track before handing off duties to the next ref. Skaters skate for several laps at a time. My heart wants this; my joints and ligaments feel more conflicted. *Who puts on roller skates—mid-career, late thirties—to smash into other people on roller skates?*

"Mama, you're awesome!" My son told me earlier today, planting a kiss on my cheek as I left the house with my skates. It reminded me of Robin Drugstores and her daughter Fire

Unicorn, spraying her down with invisible magic dust before each Heavy Metal Hookers game.

"Thanks, bud," I'd told him. Only now, I'm not feeling so awesome as my legs shake.

"Meat, urgency!" Kill says, snapping me back to attention.

Killfield, or *Kill*, is a tall skater with cropped, dyed-blonde hair. She and I serve on the Philly Roller Girls Board together, and she's one of the hardest workers I know. She's also one of the only Black skaters in the league, a reality whose implications I don't absorb clearly yet. Most of the old guard of skaters have retired—Robin Drugstores, Ivana Rock, The Cycrone. And roughly a dozen of us make up this class of new recruits.

We finish our warmups and I take a few sips of water from my bottle. Two fellow fresh meat nearby are trying out together; another skater is an oncologist with two kids. This is part of the brilliance of roller derby, people from all walks of life come together to beat each other up on roller skates. A whistle blows from across the track, followed by Kill's voice.

"Alright, pack it up, meat!" she yells.

"What does that mean?" One of my fellow cohorts whispers. "Pack it up?"

"It means get together," I whisper. I know this from watching skater practice for years.

"Gonna have you all get into a pack at the jammer line," Kill says. "When I tell you to go, you'll skate around and practice one-knee falls."

Falls are the most important part of learning to play roller derby. Mostly because they're something you do nonstop. You fall and you get back up. You get hit hard and you have to get back up. In derby, quick recovery is a must.

Turns out, falling is a talent of mine. Getting back up has been a lot harder.

"As a refresher, one-knee falls are executed like this." Kill demonstrates the drill, bending one knee down to tap the track. Then she comes back to standing on two skates. It looks deceptively easy, but this skill requires strong leg muscles, and mine are already sore.

Kill adds, "The trick is to use the momentum from skating, the momentum before you fall, to pop back up from your knees." She rises, then takes a few strides out onto the track. Using the speed as she drops, Kill puts one knee down and slides forward, like a guitar player on a stage. Then, she pulls back to standing. "Again, the key to the fall is to keep going. That momentum slides you back up," she says.

She sets us loose around the track to work on this. Only, each time I take a few quick strides, I drop down to one knee and just stick there, glued by gravity.

The key to falling is to keep going, I repeat Kill's words in my head as I fall and attempt to get back up. Giving it another go, I feel my speed slow down. It's a block I can't quite get past, my resistance to falling. I try again and throw myself onto the floor with some speed.

First, my left knee hits the floor and I waver. Without meaning to, my knee pad slides across the floor, giving just enough momentum for my right leg to pull me upwards and back to standing. Accidentally, I succeed.

"Ha!" I cry, looking around. "I did it!" The rest of the skaters are focused on their own tasks. We're all new to this, and everyone has an intense look of concentration.

Some of these folks have natural talent or abilities—roller skating, for me, doesn't come easily. And that's what I love about roller derby. You can have skaters with natural athletic talents, skating alongside women who need repetition and practice before they can fully come into their own. Roller derby needs all of these different skills and abilities. At least, that's how I see it.

After *Whip It*, *ESPN*'s *Bodies We Want*, and the establishment of WFTDA.tv, teams were overwhelmed with people wanting in. The Cycrone, Jocelyn Jenik, President of the Philly Roller Girls Board of Directors by this time, remembers the club being unprepared to deal with the influx of potential skaters.

"The difference between tryouts before *Whip It* and after was incredible," she says. "The rink was just packed with hopefuls, and we ended up having to cut massive amounts of skaters."

To prove themselves, skaters trained for several weeks to pass minimum skills requirements[41]—or, MSRs— set by the WFTDA. These skills included crossovers, falls, endurance skating, and stops. And, of course, the dreaded the twenty-seven-in-five—or, twenty seven laps around the track in five minutes.[42] Skaters were asked to demonstrate whips, pushes, weaving, and pacing, as well as blocking skills like body checks. What many programs didn't provide for was the ability for folks to learn at different paces, or in different ways.

An anonymous 2014 Op-Ed in roller derby zine *Hellarad*[43]

highlighted a growing point of contention in the sport, that top tier skaters were jumping teams to play roller derby and pushing less skilled skaters off rosters. Or, as the process came to be known, *transfergate.*

*"Dear Fuckity Fuckt**** Transfer Skater coming from a long and somewhat impressive list of leagues... Why the fuck do you really think we should let you into our league? Oh right, because YOU are an amazing skater. YOU have charisma and the crowd will love YOU. You will help our All Star team reach its wildest aspirations..."*

The main target of the venom was Oly Rollers, who penned a response.

"Hellarad, a derby zine, was particularly profane in their criticism calling the Oly Rollers 'the douchiest team in all of roller derby.'" Though this term made me snicker, their letter highlighted the competitive shifts in roller derby—Oly was a winning team, and it wanted to stay that way. So it welcomed highly-skilled transfers.

Many of those cut ended up leaving to join smaller clubs, which was challenging financially. In Philadelphia alone, we had a handful of nearby competing clubs, including Penn Jersey Roller Girls—both banked track and flat track—Atlantic Coast Roller Girls, Jersey Shore Roller Girls, and Brandywine Roller Girls. All within an hour or so drive of the city.

Again, this showed the power of the sport and its ability to bring people in. Problem was, once people were brought in, many were suddenly told they weren't good enough yet. Like I was: *You surpassed the WFTDA minimum laps in 5 minutes, however, we feel you need more time to learn basic skills before entering scrimmage… and moving on to the next round.*

When I got cut from fresh meat in late 2013, I was devastated. I'd spent several years psyching myself up to try it. By then I'd done everything else in the sport: announcing, officiating, DJ-ing, selling merch, selling beer, building WFTDA. tv. I had a WFTDA job, a title, and I was on the Board of Directors for Philly. But I didn't want special treatment; I just wanted a fair shot. Now I'd have to wait another year to try out again. Who knows where I'd be then? I decided to write an email to the fresh meat coaches.

I watched fellow skaters… whom I lapped in my 27 in 5 assessments, move on to complete the program… I attended 100% of the practices… My falls have improved since the last round. My fellow meat asked me for advice with certain things I was mastering. There was nothing within the program structure that allowed me to think I wasn't in line with expectations.

My questions were critical ones for where roller derby was in 2013: Was the point of all of this to help each skater succeed, and meet them where they're at? Was there room for all of us? Or was the goal to only take the best and let everyone else fall through the cracks? Philly's coaches acknowledged this in their response to my email.

There has been much discussion with the panel and the majority vote is in favor of giving you another chance in the way of reassessment. We will go over every skill before assessing you on it but it will be a repeat of last week's assessment. This is to take place at the beginning of practice. The panel will then convene to make a final decision.

"You petitioned your panel to assess you again?" Bloody Mary, my then-boss, had asked me incredulously when I told her what had happened. "Of course you did." Because, what else would Double H do?

As with most of Philadelphia, Philly's Liberty Belles All Stars patron saint was Rocky Balboa. The team used *Gonna Fly Now* as its rallying cry. And in this fresh meat experience, I was also starting to see something critical about myself. That sometimes urgency isn't about skating faster. It means refusing to stay down. Like so many, I'd put too much time and energy into this sport to stay down. Not when I was so close to becoming a skater that I could taste it.

Illustration by Sandra Frame,
a.k.a. Tara Armov.

individual derby

noun

---

when a blocker is blocking outside of formation, used as a last resort.

CHAPTER 20:

Danger Zone

March, 2014. Camden, New Jersey.

Three weeks later, the taste of salt on my lips is my own sweat. Like Rocky Balboa, I'm fighting to stay upright; unlike him, I'm skating in my first-ever game of roller derby on skates that are too big. Every jam I've ever announced. Every shot I've reframed. Every scrimmage I've officiated. It's all led to this moment. I'm a Cheeseskate, or a member of the C-Team.

Huffing, I swivel in front of the jammer from Strong Island—or, in the non-derby world, Long Island, New York. This is my first-ever game, my reward for petitioning the fresh meat panel to reassess me—and succeeding. Only, the jammer in my ribcage is making me rethink this reward. I'm sweating onto the top of her red helmet as Beyoncé's "Who Run the World (Girls)" thumps through the rink.

Around me, the rest of the pack is a swirl of noise and sensation: elbows, knees, grunts, sweating, pushing, yelling. It envelops me as I try to get in front of Strong Island's jammer. I roll forward, holding her back—I dig my skate wheels into the track, turning my feet to 45 degree angles to slow myself.

"Double H, get lower," I hear Kill's voice, my captain for this game, and I comply, dropping my booty. This lowers my center of gravity and helps keep me upright.

"Double H, hold her!" My teammate grunts from a few bodies away. Her voice is the only sound I hear above the din of the spectators; I can barely make out the shouts of fans.

Come on, Strong Island!

You got this, Cheeseskates!

My son is somewhere in the audience, but I can't hear him over the chaos. Secretly, I don't want him to see me fuck up. Out of the corner of my eye, I catch the flash of Philly Roller Girls cheerleaders, or *Phearleaders*, as they hop up and down with sparkly blue and red pom-poms. Maybe two hundred bodies stand around the roller rink, with our flat track drawn in blue tape on the wooden rink floor. I eye it as I'm pushed forward like a bobsled.

"I'm here, I'm here!" My teammate hollers as she slides over to me. She presses herself into my side, and together we form a seal to keep the jammer back. Her skates plow into the track like a bicycle kickstand. Our Cheeseskates jammer breaks free behind us—I only know this because I see a blur of white pass me as a double whistle sounds.

"Lead Jammer, Cheeseskates," I hear the announcer say over the same loudspeaker I once heard at my first game, seven years ago. A lot has changed. And yet, I'm still me, still here in Camden. Still with roller derby.

Strong Island's jammer groans as she presses into us. "Help," she says to her teammates, and I anticipate a hit. I turn my head to see an incoming Strong Island blocker. As she crashes into my shoulder, I steady myself against my blocking partner.

"Jammer, jammer, jammer," I hear another Strong Island blocker say as our Cheeseskates jammer sails past all of us in a flurry of skates and grunts. As she does, she eyes me to see if my teammate and I are holding New York's jammer. Since we are, she nods at me and races forward for another pass. My gut explodes with pride. I've played team sports before, but never one where the offense works so symbiotically with the defense. We're doing totally different things but working together towards the same goal.

The referee's four whistles tell me the jam is up. Strong Island's jammer pulls back from me as the jam comes to an end. My teammate and I regain our balance, purple-faced and sweating. Huffing and puffing, we drift off the track. The next line of skaters enters behind us and we high five one another as we pass.

"Oh my god, we did it," I say, sucking air at my blocking partner, my teammate.

"That was magical," she says, breathing. We hug, we sweat.

"Nice job, Cheeseskates," my coach says as we roll back to the bench. I take a sip from my water bottle as the DJ drops "Girls Just Wanna Have Fun" by Cyndi Lauper. For once, I feel this song deep in my bones. I am a girl—a thirty-six-year-old girl—playing her first-ever official game of roller derby. And I am having a shit ton of fun.

As I entered my first season as a skater I realized that not everyone in roller derby was celebrating—or feeling celebrated.

And not everyone identified as a girl. Or as a woman.

"So much of roller derby was about breaking out of stereotypes for women," shares Juliana Gonzales, a.k.a. Bloody Mary, with me. By early 2014, the WFTDA had over 230 clubs. "For women who were in a hetero structure at home, I think it felt really liberating to find a space of liberation around their femininity and their sexiness, and their strengths and badassery." Soon, this culture of nonconformity pushed our gender exploration in a new direction.

At the 2014 WFTDA Playoffs from Evansville, Indiana, WFTDA broadcast used *they/them* pronouns for skaters on air. It was something that was easy to accommodate—at least from my perspective. Only, the subsequent social media chatter was challenging, and Tweets rolled in throughout the weekend with sentiments like:

Are you saying "they" is lead jammer? #Talk2WFTDA

Using "they/them" pronouns is easy and inclusive. #Talk2WFTDA

How else should we refer to nonbinary skaters? "She/her" doesn't apply.

"[Roller derby] got blindsided by nonbinary folks completely," shares Stefanie Madison, formerly known as Kim Deal With It, Talent Coordinator for the 2014 tournament. "'If you compete in the WFTDA, you're a woman' was the directive we got from leadership at first."

Nonbinary and *genderqueer* were terms that emerged in the mid-1990s,[44] so they weren't new. But as Madison states, roller derby wasn't prepared to tackle these pronouns. Most sports wouldn't contemplate them for another decade, or some not

124

at all. So even as I was eager to showcase the sport, our own community wasn't done defining women-led spaces.

That year, the Men's Roller Derby Association, MRDA, publicly included nonbinary and gender fluid skaters, after releasing what it called the "Unisex"[45] version of the rules in 2011. "With permission from the WFTDA," their 2011 press release shared, "the MRDA modified the feminine ruleset to an inclusive, gender neutral version." JRDA, the Junior Roller Derby Association, addressed this problem by having both a women's division and an open division, which invited kids ages 6-18 to compete on mixed gender teams.

Many members were strongly aligned with the word "women;" others argued that if roller derby was about embodying your most authentic self, nonbinary community members mattered, too. Other sports—and sports media—were not only years behind us in these conversations, they were navigating a whole different culture for women. And not always a welcoming one.

Cheese Skates vs. Strong Island.
Photo credit: Joellen Leather-Urban
for Philly Roller Derby.

fresh legs

noun

---

a skater thrown into a game to relieve other more tired skaters.

CHAPTER 21:

Put Me In, Coach

May, 2014. Camden, New Jersey.

Clomp, clomp, clomp. I'm plodding up the steps to Campbell's Field. The alluring, fatty scent of Chickie's and Pete's fries draws me up each cement step. I glance at my bare legs, pale and muscular. I have roller derby to thank for the muscle, the Riversharks to thank for me being here. While the former brings me an outlet for stress, baseball somehow naturally relieves it.

Moving into my second season with the Camden Riversharks, I reach the top of the stairs and enter the press box. The breeze from the diamond comes through the open window and washes over me. My announcing partner, a man in his forties, nods with a smile. Putting my bag down, I pull out my baseball scoring book next to his laptop; my job now includes announcing radio broadcasts of games, as well as writing recaps for the website.

My new boss at the Sharks, a man in his early thirties, pops his head in to ask how it's going. We nod and my announcing partner points my way.

"She's doing great," he says. I can't help but smile at his kind words.

"We'd love to work you into pregame reporting and interviews eventually," my boss says.

"Great!" I say. My arms tingle. In roller derby, I've been doing interviews for years. I'm good at it, and I love it. This is great news.

"But the manager doesn't want you in the clubhouse, so we'll have to figure something out," he adds, as though these things are a given. My shoulders drop. A woman in the clubhouse is still a liability in 2014.

Minor league baseball—and other sports—are quick to use gender to justify inequities. *You're a woman, you can't be here.*

"Ready to record the pregame?" My partner asks. We usually record an intro to the show—since it's audio-only, I've started to script them to feel more confident. I nod.

As he hands me a stack of lineups and stats, I catch my broadcast partner's computer, open to *ESPN3*. The video player features little league baseball, and for a second I feel my face grow hot. It hits me then that children—actual children—are a more viable product for *ESPN* than women on roller skates. Putting on my headset, I'm simmering. And when I get angry, I usually get motivated.

"Women were always asked to fall in line," says former *ESPN* writer Jane McManus of her time in sports media—both at *ESPN* and other outlets. "And if you didn't fall in line, you were moved off projects." McManus, also a former jammer with Suburbia Roller Girls, understood sports media from multiple angles—both the position of women in the larger sports landscape, and the tiny piece women's roller derby had in that landscape.

In 2013, more than a decade ago, there were very few women on a sports microphone of any kind in Philadelphia. I had no idea that on a much larger scale, women like McManus were fighting the same battle. Even early *ESPN* pieces about her involvement in roller derby focused on her work-life balance as a mother, as with this 2011 article from *ESPN Front Row*.[46]

"McManus, who will cover the NFL draft this week for *ESPNNY.com* and be featured when *espnW*'s enhanced website debuts Tuesday, balances her work life with family (she's a wife and mother) and multiple practices a week." It wasn't lost on McManus that no one mentioned men having to balance families and work.

"My husband is a baseball writer himself," says *The Athletic* Enterprise Editor Emma Span, who started her career covering baseball. "People ask me all the time, 'How did you get into baseball?' And I realize he never gets asked that. Like, how does *anyone* get into baseball? They love baseball."

And gender isn't the only challenge; sports media is competitive. Former Director of Programming Todd Myers called working at *ESPN* "a grind" when I asked him about his time there. He explains, "Programming is the hub of the wheel. Everything flows through programming—sales, marketing, production. There's a lot of pressure. And the competition to be great is very stiff."

Over time, Myers shares, the composition of that

competition began to change.

"There's more women getting into sports now," says Myers, who joined *ESPN*'s programming department in 2004. When he first started, "the ratio of men to women years ago was heavily skewed to men. That's changing. But it's ultra competitive."

Jane McManus sums up the paradox of being a woman at the most competitive network in the sports industry, *ESPN*. "It comes down to, do you wanna have a job there or not?" This was the exact feedback I got in Camden. *Engage on our terms or not at all.*

Around the same time, and totally unbeknownst to me, Juliana Gonzales and our WFTDA Board President, Amanda Hull—Alassin Sane from Atlanta—were getting similar vibes from the head of the International Olympic Committee's roller sports organization. Noting our growing visibility, the parent organization for USARS had summoned the WFTDA to Rome to talk about the fast growth of roller derby. And how they wanted to *absorb it* into an Olympic pathway. The idea was intriguing, but the IOC had notoriously strict standards on gender definitions and requirements. Still, the pair went with an open mind.

"There was a bit of naivete on our part," shares Bloody in a recent chat. "Not small shop vs. big corporation; but the naivete of women presuming they would be taken seriously on their accomplishments." As I had with the Riversharks; as McManus had with *ESPN*.

"Alassin Sane and I showed up for the meeting and they very kindly and somewhat paternalistically offered to take over the sport for us," she adds, noting the WFTDA eventually declined the offer. "I said 'there are parts of this that would really be hard to navigate given our current membership structure.' But what I really meant was, 'go fuck yourself.'"

For better or for worse, roller derby, not just in my eyes, was determined to live on our own terms. No matter the cost.

The view from the press box in
old Campbell's Field, Camden, New Jersey.
Photo credit: Erica Vanstone

jammer-on-jammer action

noun

---

when a jammer plays defense against the opposing jammer.

CHAPTER 22:

The Big Show

January, 2015. Bristol, Connecticut.

"I'm here to see the Director of Programming." I smile at the guard at *ESPN*'s headquarters in Bristol, Connecticut. Peering through the metal gate, the place looks like a well-protected college campus with trim greenery on the outside. The guard inspects my ID card, scans it, and hands it back to me. He waves me through to visitor parking. This is the closest modern roller derby has ever gotten to a relationship with television. I just hope I can make it count.

After I park, *ESPN*'s Director of Programming, Todd Myers, meets me at the door. He's a tall, laid-back man with a fluid voice. I was introduced to Todd through a colleague who works at NFL Films. Extending his hand, Myers eyes my light gray blazer, matching his own.

"Glad you got the memo on our matching outfits," he says with a nod. His quip makes me laugh and I relax.

"Is this some sort of power move in sports?" I joke back. "Instead of 'dress to impress' it's 'dress like the person you're trying to impress?'" A snicker and a nod from him tells me he appears to be a decent human.

Myers guides me around the *ESPN* complex and it's huge. We walk to a dim cavern where mostly white, male editors cut highlight reels for the network's news shows. Inside the *ESPN* clip room, cubicles fan out like the audio-visual section of my college library. Each bay is stuffed with people pulling clips from tennis, hockey, curling, and cricket—which is Myers' area of focus.

I only spot one woman in this row of editors at the two dozen or so bays; I think of my volunteer highlight reel producer, Michelle Cartier—a.k.a. Atreyu. We get so much done on our shoestring budget. Here, everyone wears headphones and focuses intently on pulling content to run on various shows. Some of these sports—the Major League Baseball, the National Football League, and the National Basketball Association—have deals in place where the network pulls clips for them, mostly because they bring so many viewers, and in turn, ad revenue.

"If you send us clips, we can run them on *SportsCenter*," Myers says.

I swallow hard, trying to process. All this time and energy and money put into showcasing sports that already have their own economic engines, their own revenue drivers. Roller derby, and most women's sports, don't have this kind of support. We're told it's a matter of quality, that we're just not *watchable*. Yet in the first year of WFTDA.tv, the number of pay-per-view customers crashed the site.

"For WFTDA Championships," Myers says a few minutes later, sitting me down at a table in the network's cafeteria, "I'm thinking you need one of the network's producers."

Like every other room in the complex, the *ESPN* cafeteria is huge. The walls are dark and today's menu is displayed on hand-written boards, as though we're in a high-end bistro. He hands me a cup of black coffee and a list of producers. "In order for the network to agree to acquisitions, they like to bring in a trusted producer."

The sentence makes my nose scrunch involuntarily—our work with Joe Christensen and Blaze is solid enough to bring in about $250,000 in revenue for three years now. "We're capable of pushing out to your streaming network, though," I say, blowing across my hot coffee. "To *ESPN3*. We just need the right encoder."

"Right," Myers says. I don't know him well, but I sense he's being generous, and that I shouldn't argue with what he's telling me. "The sample you shared with me was good—and we won't even make you pay for the air time. But you do need to put that money into quality, and using a broadcast truck is the way to go, using our graphics package and show elements."

A time buy that's free. Almost like an investment. I look up from the paper cup catching the last thing he said. "We can use *ESPN*'s graphics?"

"Of course you can," he says. "That's how you can give the show polish." I hadn't thought of this, of our roller derby content, of our show with *ESPN*'s name all over it. I feel excitement and dread over having to explain this to the WFTDA Board of Directors. I scan the list of producers he hands me, a bunch of men who own satellite trucks with graphics bays and camera gear. This is the part we pay for, the price for higher quality.

He adds, gesturing towards the list, "This is your first show on our platforms, you should be focusing on getting the sport right. A package producer can help you do that, help you stay focused. They take care of the stream, you just make sure you put together incredible games."

"No big deal." I feel myself inhale deeply.

He laughs. "You wouldn't be here if I didn't think you could pull it off."

"You'd be surprised by how often competence doesn't actually get you anywhere when you're a woman in sports." I'd spent years trying to build broadcast to a place where I could even have this conversation with *ESPN*. I had to be honest about how hard it had been.

"Hopefully, I can change that and help get roller derby its big break." He smiles, then drops his expression. "Wait, is it bad luck to say something like 'break a leg' in roller derby?"

"I don't know, actually," I admit, half-smiling. "I don't think it's like theater."

"Well, let's err on the side of caution and say we're not breaking anything."

I nod. No more breaking. No more failure. Only incredible games—our way.

What I didn't realize in 2015 was how critical having an advocate like Todd Myers is for a small sport like roller derby, especially a women's sport. When roller derby first started talking to *ESPN* in 2009, it was with Todd Myers himself.

At that time, Myers tells me, "we were inundated with

people pitching us. The way that we had to find the folks who were real was to say, 'Look, we're going to charge a modest time buy, maybe five thousand dollars.'" To get those fees waived, or to get a deal, Myers adds, you needed "an internal champion and to sell someone who's higher up the food chain." In 2009, roller derby didn't have that advocate. But by the time I met with him in 2015, we did.

Women's sports have always had an even harder time finding a champion. Although, as *ESPN* writer Jane McManus admits, the network "has done more to promote women's sports than any other entity." She points to *espnW*, the affiliate site and brand of the main site, *ESPN.com*. "No other sports property has a women's brand. [Yet] *ESPN* has also done more to hold women's sports back. Because they hold the rights to and don't show certain events. Or they had the rights and didn't promote the sport, like the WNBA and women's college basketball."

Not only was I representing a women's sport, I was showcasing a contact sport played in tattoos and lipstick. The further I pushed into professional sports, the more I was confronted by its realities. And the more I realized: professional sports and the mainstream media were absolutely, unequivocally threatened by the likes of us. And some of the worst—and the best—outcomes of that misalignment were yet to come.

Speaking of misalignments, the force of a hammer smashes me directly on the nose. Months later, I recoil from my opponent's shoulder, tasting warm liquid rolling onto my lips. At first, I think it's mucus as it spills onto the track below me at June's East Coast Derby Extravaganza. Then I see a fist-sized puddle of crimson around my skate wheels. *That's blood—that's my blood.*

The last time I saw that much of my own blood, I was birthing another human. Today, I'm skating against Madison's B Team, a collection of tall, fair-haired, muscular Midwesterners with an apparently loose grasp on legal game play. A howling pain emerges in my sinuses.

I don't have time to debate the action's legality as a new thought emerges: *My nose is broken.* I fall to my knees, grasping my nose. A frenzy of whistles erupts around me.

"Double H," I hear my coach's voice, then feel her arm under my shoulder. She guides me to the bench. Out of the corner of my eye I see a flash of bright yellow, as the vests of the EMTs make their way over. All I can think of is getting patched up so I can get back on the track—even as a handful of volunteers mop up my blood.

"She fucking high blocked me," I choke, limping forward, not out of pain but out of rage. I'm holding back my own blood with my fingers. A man's latex-gloved fingers grasp my hands, but I'm unwilling to let go of my own face for fear of what's underneath.

"This is why we tell you—don't block solo," she says.

I groan, "I know, I know." But she's right. As a last resort, I was facing backwards to catch the jammer and I got nailed. Blocking alone is a no-go when you can avoid it.

"Here, I got it," the EMT says, coaxing me to release my grip. When I do, I see stars for a moment, then blink them away. Trying to calm down, I don't speak but take a mental checklist of my other body parts, which seem to be intact.

"Is it broken?" I breathe towards the EMT.

"Dunno yet," he says, dabbing an ice pack wrapped in gauze on my face. "We'll find out once I get the bleeding to stop."

I mentally sift through the handful of pertinent birthdays of people in my life, and I am confident I don't have a concussion—at least not a severe one.

"Fucking high block." I feel every part of my body grow hot with anger.

"Tilt your head back for me?" The diligent EMT keeps working, despite my sputtering. The thing I've been terrified of this whole time, injuring myself playing roller derby, has happened. Though the pain isn't any worse than childbirth, all of it is terrifying, yet somehow manageable. Almost exhilarating.

"Can I get back in the game?" I ask in the direction of the EMT.

"Uh, seeing how I'm about thirty seconds away from taking you to the ER in an ambulance, I'm gonna say no," he says. I can't tell if he's joking. He gingerly packs a tampon-like wad of gauze into each nostril, wiping blood from the sides of my nose.

"Not broken," the EMT says, removing the ice pack from my face, using his thumb and forefinger to softly pat at the bones of my nose. "Well, *probably* not. You're just a gusher. In a day or two, you'll know for sure."

"Does it hurt?" my son asks, squinting into my face an hour

or so later. My nine-year-old wears a red Philly Roller Girls Juniors shirt with the name "Catman" on the back. Catman inspects the blood crusting around my nose.

"No, I'm alright," I say, trying to put on a brave face. But I can't get much past him as I sit down next to him at the announcer's table on the Sportsplex mezzanine. He bunches his face.

"Mom, that looks bad," he says.

"I promise I'm good. You excited to announce this game with me?" He nods.

Catman is my nine year-old announcing partner for one of Philly's juniors games. We're on the broadcast call together: new junior roller derby skater and… his mom. But Catman's been watching the sport his whole life. To say he knows a thing or two is an understatement as we make our way through the game—Philly Juniors vs. Ithaca.

"I can't believe this score, this is such a high score for these teams, Catman," I say.

"It is 154, that's Philly, and Ithaca has 130," he says.

"Before we go into halftime, you said you feel that Ithaca might not be trying their hardest. What do you think they need to try harder to do, do you think?"

"Their *believance*."

I pause for a half second, making sure I heard him correctly. "Their *believance*?"

"Yeah, they're not believing that they can have that many points," he says. His frankness makes me bite my lip in glee. I've forgotten that my face is bashed in and it hurts, but I can't stop myself from smiling. My son just invented a word. And it's awesome. *Believance.*

"So, you're saying it's their mental game?"

"Yeah, they need to believe they can score."

"Alright, their *believance*," I say, nodding. And I watch the internet explode with my son's display of cuteness.

#Talk2WFTDA I think we all need to have more #Believance, Catman.

#Believance #Talk2WFTDA Sports quote for the ages!

For the first time, though not the last, roller derby rips me open and stitches me back together. Lovingly. Brutally. And all in one day.

Illustration by Sandra Frame,
a.k.a. Tara Armov.

power slide

noun

---

a stop that's similar to a hockey stop, that requires a sharp turn that resolves in a sideways, one-footed slide.

CHAPTER 23:

Out Here in the Fields

November, 2015. Minneapolis, Minnesota.

"How's everyone enjoying the best roller derby action on the planet?"
John Maddening, Minnesota's venue announcer, is in his element. The tall Midwesterner with faded aqua hair and a plaid suit hypes the crowd. The Roy Wilkins Auditorium—*the Roy*—is his home and he coaxes spectators into a frenzy with ease. I stand alone a few yards away from him next to our two broadcast announcers and a monitor. Headphones on, I hear Blaze's crew in our rented truck.

"Ready camera two…. go camera two…"

Rose City's Wheels of Justice take on Gotham Girls Roller Derby All Stars for the Hydra. Gotham enters the game as a five-time WFTDA champion. The Roy is ablaze, lit up like a bonfire with the energy of these two teams.

But I have tunnel vision. I'm not looking at the track, nor the five thousand or so screaming fans around it. Nor the camera platforms, cables leading to the satellite truck out of the loading bay, or the frenzied benches packed with sweaty skaters. I'm looking at the monitor's rectangle, what viewers see as they watch roller derby live on *ESPN3*.

With under five minutes left, Loren Mutch steps out to jam for Rose City against veteran Gotham jammer Bonnie Thunders. Mutch's face is sweaty and deadpan, telling me maybe she feels the weight of all this, too. The score is 179 Gotham and 166 Rose, with just three and half minutes on the clock. And the *ESPN* logo is over it all.

We're pushing out our live, branded stream to *ESPN3* and every bone in my body is on fire. After the whistle, Loren Mutch scores four points for Rose and calls off the jam—good, old fashioned *hit it and quit it* roller derby. This puts her team in striking distance, with a 179–170 score. Gotham wisely decides to call a timeout to reset their strategy.

"Bonnie Thunders there, always looking just calm, cool, and collected," Mike Chexx, the play-by-play broadcaster says, eyeing Gotham's bench. On the monitor, I watch the director, our own roller derby director, Benjamin Doyle, talking to the camera operators in my headset. He picks a crowd shot with Gotham fans, holding a sign that says, "Hard, Smart, Together!"

"Camera three, widen out a bit. Perfect. Ready three? Go camera three…"

Rose's next jammer, a tall, muscular skater named Scald Eagle, is sent out against Bonnie Thunders, Gotham's go-to. After the whistle, Eagle grabs lead jammer status. Roller derby photographers snap away, lights flashing.

"Scald Eagle barrels through the pack, five point scoring pass, Rose City," Mike Chexx growls louder into the microphone. Seconds later, the jam winds to a conclusion. Rose City now has the lead, with an incredible 193–187. The crowd folds

itself into a wall of sound, a wave crashing down on the Roy, sweeping everyone up in the ecstasy of a lead change.

"*Camera four, stay on the bench...*"

I look from the monitor to the track—roller derby looks incredible from every angle.

"*It is insane in here right now,*" I hear Chexx holler on the broadcast call. And I know this is a good time to remind folks what just happened in this game.

"*Erica for director, can we bring up those stats?*" I ask the director in my headset.

"*Absolutely, camera four, get me a static wide. And, go for graphics.*"

The game's stats fade onto the screen, showing a neck-and-neck bout between these teams. In my mind, the outcome here doesn't matter. It's not the result, it's not the final score. Not even the winner or *not-winner* of the game. It's the feeling I want to share, here—the feeling I felt, walking into that very first roller derby game in Camden, NJ all those years ago. The feeling of falling in love.

The DJ suddenly drops The Who's "Baba O'Riley," its opening piano chords amplifying the intensity across the auditorium. The whistle starts the jam, releasing Mutch, who battles four Gotham blockers all the way to the far straight-away. Gotham's Bonnie Thunders suddenly grabs lead—but this is the last jam. Because Gotham is trailing, they won't call off the jam until they've made up the twelve points they need to win. The game is down to the final seconds.

Both Loren Mutch and Bonnie Thunders get stuck behind the pack, neither team scoring. Mutch looks over to her bench—her coaches jump up and down, beaming. Rose City knows they have the points to win this game, that the clock is on their side. That their defense just needs to hold Bonnie Thunders. And they do.

"Eight seconds, crowd chanting down the jam clock," Mike Chexx hollers into the mic. *"Our unofficial final Rose City two-oh-six, Gotham Girls Roller Derby, one-ninety-five."* And with that, the Hydra has a new home.

Watching from the sidelines, I have what I think is the greatest game in the history of roller derby captured on video. This wasn't just a win for roller derby, it was a win on *ESPN3, inside* a billion dollar sports machine. And if these viewers didn't know flat track roller derby before, they know it now. The revolution may not be televised. But it sure as fuck just got streamed on the worldwide leader of sports.

The *ESPN3* broadcast of the 2015 WFTDA Championship game revealed an incredible and measurable impact in our community. Articles about us were featured in the *Austin Business Journal*, *espnW*, *Sports Video Group*, and *Bustle*.

"A broader audience for roller derby could revolutionize not just the sport, but the way female athletes are seen and treated," writes *Bustle* journalist[47] and skater Amanda Williams. Which is exactly the way I saw it, too. Watching Rose City skaters celebrate on the bench that night—their sweaty high fives, their tears of relief and joy—everything we'd put into this sport felt validated and real and important.

Not only was *ESPN3* a win, but other victories were

unrolling the same week. Our games incorporated *they/them* pronouns and included nonbinary and openly transgender skaters. All of this, and the WFTDA finally released a new statement[48] on gender.

An individual who identifies as a woman, intersex woman, and/or gender expansive may skate with a WFTDA charter team if women's flat track roller derby is the version… with which they most closely identify… With these words, the WFTDA stated outright its inclusion of transgender women and nonbinary members. The response is echoed on Twitter.

Hell yeah, WFTDA! #Talk2WFTDA

WeFTDA is what we should call ourselves!

Jane McManus covered it all in a piece published in *espnW*[49] in the days following the 2015 Championships, "Transgender Athletes Find Community, Support In Roller Derby."

"[I]deas of identity are radically evolving," writes McManus. "When it comes to gender, people are able to decide who they are and how they want to be seen. The idea of a binary, of an either/or when it comes to gender is also evolving."

At the end of the day, this is what flat track roller derby was trying to showcase to the world on *ESPN3* with the WFTDA Championships—our brand of sport. Sport that said "yes" to outsiders like us when almost every other sport on the planet said "no." Sport that said women can be soft and strong, vulnerable, and badass.

The legendary Bonnie Thunders, 2015.
Photo credit: Paul Robertson/Preflash Gordon.

non-derby direction

noun

---

skating clockwise, opposite the direction roller derby is played.

CHAPTER 24:

Blood on the Track

Summer, 2016. Feasterville, Pennsylvania.

The WFTDA and [Fédération Internationale de Roller Sports] have engaged in a series of conversations... discussing roller derby's evolution and expansion, ruleset, governance, competition, and aspirations for further growth. After returning to its membership to explore various partnerships and collaborations with FIRS... WFTDA's member leagues overwhelmingly wish to remain autonomous...

Around the same time as I was putting roller derby on *ESPN3*, the WFTDA wasn't just innovating gender policy—it was also flipping off the International Olympic Committee. In an open letter to the community just before Championships, Bloody proclaims the WFTDA's independence. But I know she's tired; advocacy work is exhausting. Which is why I'm not surprised when she tells me she's leaving in a conversation mid-2016.

Bloody is one of the guiding lights of the WFTDA, of roller derby—both on and off the track. To lose her in a position of leadership is a huge blow, especially to me. She's strong and thoughtful, smart and gutsy. Losing her makes me feel like I'm not working hard enough to make broadcasting more lucrative, but I don't tell her this.

"You should apply for my job," she says.

"Me?" I'm still reeling from the idea that she's leaving.

"You'd be great at it. You're sort of a mad scientist and you get things done."

"Mad scientist. Is this a good thing?"

"In roller derby, yes." I don't feel like it's a good thing, though. I feel like I'm often more of a lone wolf. Even as a teammate, I'm still learning how to work with other people. And I'm polarizing. People either love me or hate me, especially on the internet.

Could I be in charge of the WFTDA? Could I write open letters or advocate or write policy? I tried to envision myself in this position, what kind of leader I'd actually be. Or, what kind of mother a position like this would make me—one less present than I already felt?

I considered this idea and its magnitude. And how the magnitude of the sport was getting larger, whether I liked it or not.

Heading into 2016, the WFTDA had expanded to 385 clubs around the world, including twenty-two in the UK and Ireland, six in Central and South America, thirty-eight in Europe, three in Japan, and seventeen in Australia and New Zealand. From the humble thirty or so clubs that existed right before I walked in the door in Camden, under Bloody Mary the organization saw a 424% increase in membership.

What's more, the composition of membership in the WFTDA was just as impressive, clubs that were, "51% owned by league members who identify as women or gender expansive," according to the WFTDA's membership requirements,[50] and "(m)anaged by at least 67% league members who identify as women or gender expansive."

As the WFTDA's tagline suggested, we were an entry point for all kinds of folks looking for something new and meaningful: *Real. Strong. Athletic. Revolutionary.* WFTDA.tv had started to broadcast games, not just on *ESPN3*, but also on our own platforms in Spanish and French. We'd opened conversations with BBC Sports and other global outlets. Flat track roller derby had seemingly taken over the world under Bloody's leadership.

And these were huge skates to fill. Her job included a lot of moving parts for the next leader to come in and manage. Derby was being seen, not just by ESPN, but by all kinds of new eyeballs across the globe. To keep the momentum going, our next moves were critical. So was choosing the right person for the job.

brace

noun

---

a blocking position whose job is to hold a wall steady and in place.

CHAPTER 25:

That's My Teammate

Late Summer, 2017. Philadelphia, Pennsylvania.

"Did you get the Executive Director job, Double H?" one of my well-meaning teammates asks me on the bench as we're between games at a Saturday night game in Maryland against DC Roller Derby's B-Team. I guzzle water and shake my head.

"No," I exhale. Turning away, I want to be excited for the woman they hired, the first woman of color in WFTDA leadership, a weightlifter with no ties to roller derby. Cassie Haynes is a clear top choice for this role, hailing from a CrossFit-adjacent sport called National Pro Grid League. Fresh eyes are a good thing. I'm just not sure the culture is ready for an outsider to run such a behemoth of an organization. It's a feeling akin to wanting to tidy your house before a housekeeper arrives. And I'm not quite sure why I feel this way.

As my bench manager motions me onto the track for the next jam, I reason with myself. *You weren't ready to be a leader, anyway.* I tell myself this, though I'm not sure I believe it. Our new ED comes with some great connections like CBS Sports—which may be good for all of us.

"Five seconds!" the jam timer in the center of the track hollers. I crouch, facing the jammer and holding the shoulders of my teammates behind me. I'm the brace and my job is to hold the wall into place in front of the jammer by facing backwards.

While I do, I talk myself into feeling like I've dodged a bullet. *You're working on bringing roller derby to the big time. Do you really want to be running everything else at the same time as an Executive Director?*

The jammer crashes into my wall.

"Get on her, get on her." I snap back to the moment, urging the two blockers to get their hips to maintain contact with the jammers. "Hips down... left... left... pull up a little..." DC's jammer is locked in what we call the pocket, exactly where we want her. On the track and off, I know I need to be patient and stick to my plan: patient blocking, world domination through broadcast. What I don't know yet is that not getting the job exactly doesn't mean I'm off the leadership hook. Not yet.

"There's no way that something that was designed for twelve clubs could scale without a strategy that contemplated scaling from the beginning," says Cassie Haynes, who would serve as the Executive Director of the WFTDA from January through November 2017. Walking into a job running an amateur sport with 40,000 constituent bosses, a hundred or so high level volunteers, an elected Board, and a handful of staff members was daunting for Haynes—as it would have been for anyone. It was growth I hadn't even fully processed because I'd been with the sport almost from the beginning. And it wasn't the only thing that wasn't visible to me.

Haynes says, "Decision-making was often designed around people, specific individuals, on their personalities. A governance structure based on whims and personalities is not sound. If you continue to build on top of a foundation, what do you get? You get a Hydra." The Hydra, of course, is the WFTDA's top trophy, a pewter roller skate on a stand. Haynes' point is well made. Structures not designed to scale are often destined to fail.

"But from the get-go, I thought the work was cool and I wanted to be good at it and make a difference. I think I was naive enough to be like, yeah, we can do this. We'll be able to build capacity and move revenue. We just need new leadership in place."

Yet, almost from her moment of hire, unbeknownst to the rest of us, Haynes was stepping into a system designed out of growth that was explosive and complicated; some pieces managed by staff, some by volunteers.

"Looking back on it now, I have a whole set of language and tools for reflection, being several years removed," she shares. "Particularly as a Black woman. I look back at some of the things that happened and at the moment I wouldn't have ascribed racial context to, but having a much stronger understanding, the signs were there."

When I first met Haynes, she confided in me: "Roller derby is like a church. Like some sort of evangelical church."

Without thinking, I'd responded, "No, you mean a cult." It was a joke, but only halfway. The uncomfortable silence that followed told us we weren't incorrect.

"There are tens of thousands of individuals that are invested in this on a level that is cult-like," Haynes confides in me now. "Yet, the fact that this entire sport was powered by a half dozen people and a mountain of volunteer labor—that's not a sound structure. I was like, what did I get myself into?" And while Haynes grappled with these questions, I kept doing what I knew how to do—crafting stories, reframing cameras, pushing the sport forward. Flaws and all.

Angel City vs. Arch Rival, 2017.
Photo credit: Paul Robertson/Preflash Gordon.

fan engagement

noun

---

the types of games used during sporting events to keep fans excited.

CHAPTER 26:

By the Fans, For the Fans

Summer 2017. Philadelphia, Pennsylvania.

"Did you say... *ESPN2*? Like, not internet streaming but actual television?" I'm on a conference call mid-summer with *ESPN*'s programming manager and two of her producers. I'm trying to temper my expectations, yet here's a moment I've been working towards for years—televised roller derby. Maybe even as a pipe dream more than a reality.

"Yes, we think with a few production improvements, roller derby is ready for live broadcast on the network's secondary channel, *ESPN2*. On linear television."

Taking flat track roller derby from the internet to television is a big deal, although the lines between the two are becoming increasingly blurred with improvements in technology. Then, it occurs to me that the program manager said something else I need to loop back on.

"Wait, did you say *live* to network television?" I ask. Our streams are put out live, but at best, I'd been told when a network moves a show to television, it's likely to be taped and edited.

"Absolutely," she says. "We think you're pretty much ready."

Pretty much. Two technical producers from the network weigh in on what it would take to get us the rest of the way to network quality: a production truck with a graphics bay, an encoder link direct to the network's control room, announcers approved by their team. Everything here is expensive, but doable. And I hadn't even asked for it. *ESPN* came to us.

"The timing of Championships should be between NFL games, so it works for everyone on our end," she says. "We think you could pull decent ratings in that time slot."

"That sounds great," I hear myself say.

Ratings. The holy grail of metrics. If roller derby has ratings, we *exist*. At least in sports terms. We're no longer simply, as a certain sports blogger calls us, *whores on wheels.*

I ask if I can have more ratings data to bring back to potential sponsors. *ESPN2* would mean a significant number of eyeballs for roller derby, our business partners included— roller skate companies, gear manufacturers. Others hop off the call, and the program manager puts us on hold to get some information, leaving me and a technical producer alone to make small talk.

We chat for a moment, then suddenly the tone of his voice deepens.

"Hey, can I ask you a question?" Experience has taught me that when a man prefaces a question like this, what follows is never good.

"Sure, what's your question?" I indulge him.

"Is roller derby *real?*"

My filter for this kind of bullshit is changing. And I can tell because the question causes me to laugh out loud. Instead of feeling a tight, gnawing in my gut, now I almost feel embarrassed—for *him*.

"Yes, it's real," I say.

"I just keep thinking of roller derby from the 80s. You know, where they got into fights? Punching each other like wrestling?"

We've been on the network's streaming platform for more than two years, on *ESPN3*. A network for sports. We've even been on *SportsCenter*. And he's one of the most active, well-versed technical producers at the network, whose knowledge will help make this show look *professional*. And yet, he's clearly never seen us.

"It's real," I say. "Every bit of it."

When the call ends, I sit at my desk and look out across the street and into the courtyard of a neighboring apartment complex. The family living on the ground floor is playing soccer with their young, blond son. I'm reminded of me and Catman; my son's own brilliance on the mic: *Believance*. The idea of putting roller derby on a level playing field with a sport like soccer feels unreal. Finally, a *level playing field*. That's all I want. For myself and for roller derby.

While I was navigating *ESPN2*, Cassie Haynes was trying to find a way to balance what she saw as a sport completely overgrown and unruly. The impulse to try to fix it all was alluring.

"Coming from that West Coast 'bro' vibe in CrossFit," Haynes shares with me, "I was like, roller derby's gonna be so much better—I'm working with women, I'm working with queer people. I'm working with progressive people. All of those things I didn't feel in CrossFit."

By the time Haynes took the helm, the WFTDA had almost 400 clubs globally, with nearly 40,000 skaters, officials, and volunteers. Each club, or league, had a voice in flat track's governance. Yet, voting by club took a long time; sometimes votes didn't pass at all. Cassie's vision was to restructure the org into something more responsive and streamlined; less dependent on slow-moving debate and processing, more nimble and able to serve quickly.

"Imagine a functional, efficient governance and decision-making structure from the bottom up." Haynes approached the organization with several ideas about streamlining membership. "I thought that was possible while I was there, so that's what kept me motivated."

Meanwhile, I kept going in my conversations with *ESPN2*. What neither of us saw coming was how our two biggest concerns—broadcast visibility and structural reform—were about to collide head on.

revolving door

noun

---

when a team continuously loses
skaters to the penalty box.

CHAPTER 27:

Red Letter Day

September, 2017. Kent, Washington.

"About eleven more seconds on the period call than the jam clock," says Justice Feelgood Marshall, former *DNN* blogger and my co-announcer. We're in the final two minutes of a tense game: Windy City from Chicago vs. 2x4 from Buenos Aires, Argentina—the first South American team at a WFTDA Playoff.

On the track below, Lula Zan grabs lead for 2x4 and calls off the jam, putting her team ahead 163–131—an electric turn of events. We sit perched above the arena in a broadcast booth.

"Dos Por Cuatro is kind of forcing Windy City's hand," I say, "They only have the official review left." With thirty seconds to go, Windy needs a hit-it-and-quit-it jam but they don't get the lead. Instead, Rayo from 2x4 ducks around the outside line to take it.

"Lead jammer goes to Rayo and that's going to be the game!" Justice growls.

As the final whistles sound, I glance at social media. Tweets are rolling in about both this historic game and our *ESPN2* announcement. Putting Champs on television is a huge deal, and so is the first South American team at a Playoff. So far, so good this season.

Si Dos Por Cuatro F*#@ yeah!

#Talk2WFTDA *World domination!*

ESPN2 and a South American win! Roller derby takin over! What about the rest of the world? ESPN doesn't mean shit in Europe.

I groan. We're spending forty grand or so, paid for out of our previous pay-per-view earnings, to produce a show that's only going to be televised in the United States. Folks outside the U.S. can still access it on WFTDA.tv. But here, viewers will need cable, or a subscription, to be able to watch *ESPN2*— either on a television, or through the internet. Though it's framed as linear television, it still involves a paywall. A barrier to watching the sport. The tradeoffs for visibility are worth it.

"Got a sec?" Cassie Haynes touches me on the shoulder as I finish cleaning up at the broadcast booth. She's only been in the Executive Director job for a few months and this is one of the first times we've worked together in person. She nods me over to a locker room.

"So, I'm leaving," she says.

My jaw drops. "But you just got here."

"I don't think this is the best fit for me."

She tells me how isolated she's felt. How roller derby can feel very insular, and that the sport doesn't seem ready for some of the structural changes she's looking to make. Plus, being a non-skater is also pretty isolating—this is a feeling I know firsthand. I swallow my own mix of guilt and sudden opportunity.

"What about an interim?" I blurt out. "I could put a plan together to take that on."

"You, specifically?"

Years ago, I pitched Bloody Mary on a broadcast empire; today it's the organization.

"I don't hate the idea of making you interim," she says, half smiling.

I can't see it clearly yet, but Cassie leaving is a warning sign. A signal of cracks in the foundation we'd all taken for granted—the culture, the way things were built. All I can see is that roller derby will finally be on television, and that I could also be at the helm. I'm not thinking about the weight of either. Not yet.

"I had a lot of feelings on the use of volunteer labor," says Cassie Haynes. In Cassie's mind, this was only as sustainable as people's desire to do free work—like I did for the first few seasons of broadcast. Also concerning to her was the glacial speed of decision-making. And change.

"Not unrelated," Haynes adds, "are the racial dynamics in roller derby, which is a white sport." Lots of these dynamics played out in microaggressions—for example, reports began to surface around officials who were accused of assessing more penalties against Black and Brown skaters than their white counterparts.

"Roller derby always touted itself as a very inclusive sport," shares Stefanie Madison, former head of Talent Management for the WFTDA. "But it's only for white cis women. For trans women or women of color to challenge that perception was a very big deal." A big deal that Haynes was not prepared to take on alone, nor should she have had to.

The idea the roller derby *wanted* to be inclusive but didn't quite know how to do it well was baked into its structure from the beginning.

"We were constantly trying to understand what the majority of skaters… wanted," says Hydra, a.k.a. Jennifer Wilson, one of the original architects of the sport. "But there were very loud voices that made their unpopular opinions very well known."

Sometimes these loud voices forced much-needed change, like gender policy. Or, frankly, broadcast. And almost everyone took to social media to express discontent. Which was often. Democracy and its function was a critical building block for the sport of roller derby. However, that democracy was often shaped by the loudest voices of individuals with opinions— mine included.

expulsion

noun

---

when a skater is removed from the game for posing a serious physical threat, or unsporting behavior.

CHAPTER 28:

Judgment Day

October, 2017. Philadelphia, Pennsylvania.

"Mom, are we starting on skates or off skates?" I'm standing in Philly Roller Derby's warehouse space, preparing to coach the juniors' session. Several dozen kids—including mine—put on roller derby gear near the track.

"On skates, son!" I yell in his direction. "On the track in five minutes, please." I turn back to my phone and read. *In spite of immense progress towards more sustainable practices and structures and fierce confidence in the WFTDA Leadership Team, it is time for me to move on.*

This is Cassie Haynes' formal resignation email, coming just weeks after our conversation outside of Seattle.

On November 8, Erica Vanstone will step into the role of Interim Executive Director for twelve months, during which a search will be conducted for a permanent ED.

This is good news—it's incredible news. And it's also awful news. It doesn't feel right to take over a job someone found miserable. I want roller derby to be a welcoming place for everyone. And I know now that it's not. As I gear up to pass along my near-ten-years of knowledge to kids, I feel uneasy about all of this.

"What are we working on today, Double H?" Another child asks.

Ranging in ages, many of these kids have bright, dyed hair, rainbow stockings, and decorated helmets. Looking across the group, I realize roller derby's aesthetic has transformed. Our crew includes kids who are Asian, Black, Latinx, and Indigenous. A few of the helmets have stickers with *they/them* written on gray tape to remind coaches of their pronouns.

Junior roller derby is hopeful; adults can be challenging.

"We're gonna start with one-knee falls," I say, pocketing my phone. Rolling onto the track, I use my momentum to tap a knee down on the track, then pop back up again—just like Holden Killfield taught me. I hear a yawn behind me and turn to catch my son staring at the ceiling. He pushes his mouth guard in and out with his tongue, leaning an arm on one of his friends. These kids have been skating for almost as long as I have and they're far better at it. Attention spans are questionable.

Skating up to him, I ask, "Son, you paying attention?"

"Yes, Mom," he says, eyes aimed at the ceiling, "one-knee falls." His response makes me laugh. I rest my helmet against his helmet, bringing myself nose-to-nose with him.

"Could you at least pretend to pay attention?" I ask. "I know I'm not as cool as the ceiling and all." My words force a smile from him.

"Sorry, Mom. Yes." I hold a hand out towards the track, urging him to take his turns with the drill. He's at the age where

I have to trust that I've done the best I can, as a mom and as a coach. Then trust him to fall and get back up.

"I used to say I had ten thousand bosses," says Juliana Gonzales, a.k.a. Bloody Mary, speaking about the pressures of running the WFTDA. "The voice of the people was always very important to me, and a point of tension had been economic disadvantage, racial and equity type stuff. Roller derby's a little bit weak on those points." Thus, the stakes for the role were already high. Then they got even higher.

That week, *ESPN* emailed me a request I hadn't anticipated but probably should have: a list of skater names.

FCC guidelines were always a factor with the network's platforms, so this is nothing new. After Seattle and the final Division One Playoff, we knew exactly which teams were headed to Championships, leaving us with a list of all the skaters whose names might need to be reviewed. I emailed *ESPN* back.

"As requested, we have a list of the probable teams and skaters who could be making it to that final game on Sunday. We put our notes in here about the names we'd recommend switching out. Let us know if anything looks potentially inflammatory to you?"

I attached a spreadsheet with the rosters. Most of the names should have been familiar to the network, names like *Sexy Slaydie, Bonnie Thunders, Rachel Rotten*, and *Ima BlowBya*. Derby names were part of the brand--they knew that when they came to us. Sure, a few names were cheeky or PG-13. But to me, none of them crossed a line. What I didn't understand was that in sports, the lines are constantly being redrawn. How power over names and narratives, even who gets to lead the conversation, is always being negotiated.

Rose City vs. Denver, 2018.
Photo credit: Paul Robertson/Preflash Gordon.

jammer in

verb

---

a term used to say the opposing
jammer is back from the
penalty box.

CHAPTER 29:

The Final Countdown

November, 2017. Philadelphia, Pennsylvania.

I have a few other things I'd like to discuss with you. The next morning on Monday, I read these words in an email from *ESPN. Is there a time that's good for you later today?*

It's the end of October, less than a week before the 2017 WFTDA Championships. Everything is booked or in process. I am not sure what these few other things she's referring to, but the fact that she doesn't include them in the email makes my stomach hurt.

"So, we're not going to go forward with broadcasting the WFTDA Championship game live on *ESPN2*," she says. My stomach drops. It's a week from the show. I can't believe she's saying this. "We'll review the tape and decide if it runs after the fact."

"What do you mean?" I ask. "I don't understand. You guys wanted us, you asked us, not the other way around." I'm glad we're talking on the phone so she can't see me pulling a napkin from under a stack of papers and wicking away a sudden rush of tears.

174

"It's not you," she says. "It has nothing to do with you. Or roller derby."

Heat rises across the back of my neck as the program manager explains how a new show on *ESPN*, a collaboration with Barstool Sports, caused controversy when Tweets from Barstool's founder surfaced with sexist comments. The discourse on Twitter, and the subsequent fallout, caused the network to pull the plug on all new content being produced for the time being. This was news to me as she tells me *ESPN* now has a strict review process in place for all shows that haven't run before or been vetted.

"Hang on," I say. "We *have* been vetted. We've run on your streaming platform before. For like two years. We've been on *SportsCenter*." This doesn't feel real. The agreement, the contract, allows for the network to cancel the broadcast. But not like this.

My stomach is in knots. I'd advocated for this deal. I'd vouched for the team and the expense, more than $40,000. This wasn't just a professional failure, it felt personal.

The WFTDA booked a transmission truck with a full editing and production bay, graphics generator, and package producer; elements they demanded we use. I couldn't stop thinking of all the people who believed in this; people I convinced. Blaze Streaming, the producers and directors, my teammates, my coworkers, the WFTDA Board. They all followed me up this hill. Now there was nothing at the top.

I can hear genuine guilt in her voice because I know what it sounds like. I've felt it often enough. "Maybe I can get the network to agree to run this live on *ESPN3*. You'd still have to agree to name changes, but this way it's not all a waste."

Yeah. Not all a waste. Yet, that's exactly how it feels.

When *ESPN* pulled the plug on us, I hadn't been paying much attention to anything outside of roller derby, especially not to the Barstool Sports controversy. *ESPN* personality Sam Ponder Steele wasn't too thrilled that the network had brought in Barstool, whose social media accounts had a history of being sexist. Steele Tweeted a screenshot of a post from Barstool[51] founder Dan Katz.

"Your entire career and livelihood is based on appealing to guys like me and blogs like ours… Go [expletive] yourself."

The backlash was swift and it forced *ESPN* to cancel both Barstool's *Barstool Van Talk* show and every other so-called unvetted show. Including us.

None of this had anything to do with roller derby. But the fallout cost us time and energy. The part that stung the most was the spin. *Sports Illustrated* quoted an anonymous ESPN staffer saying, "'There is quiet satisfaction that there are some values that transcend business operations.'"

ESPN fired a misogynist and quietly shelved a feminist sport. I was furious.

Still, I put in a last-ditch effort and petitioned *ESPN* to fight for us to at least be live on *ESPN3*. I owed roller derby that fight as I fired off another email to the producer.

"During the past week, we've been asked to review names, review uniforms, review platforms. Again, even a month ago this would have been workable for us. One week from the show is

not just "causing problems," it is costing us a great deal of money and trust."

For the first time, I understood what it meant to stand at the edge of a cliff you'd built for yourself. But if I was headed over, I was sure as hell gonna make some noise on the way down.

Sam Ponder ✓
@sam_ponder

Follow

I was wrong in thinking @BarstoolBigCat wrote that article & called me a slut repeatedly. He just continuously laughed along. It was the PRESIDENT of @barstoolsports who said these things. Happy to clarify.

3:51 AM · 17 Oct 2017

Sam Ponder and the Barstool Sports debacle.
Photo credit: X (formerly Twitter).

ghost points

noun

---

blockers in the penalty box, who count as points after a jammer passes the rest of the pack; also known as "box points."

CHAPTER 30:

The Greatest Story Never Told

November, 2017. Philadelphia, Pennsylvania.

"You're not actually going to do it, are you?" A tall skater, Bicepsual, folds her muscular arms, looking me up and down in the hallway of a university arena in North Philadelphia. It's eight o'clock the Friday night of Championship weekend. Victorian Roller Derby League's blocker eyes me through short, sandy curls. Standing with Cassie Haynes, Bicepsual, and Victoria's coach, I look around at all three of them, one by one.

"How can they censor my name?" Bicepsual repeats. "It's not vulgar, it's a representation of a sexual orientation." Bicepsual is one of the roller derby names in red in that *ESPN* spreadsheet, a name the network wants to censor for the weekend's streaming broadcast. They'll agree to *ESPN3* if we relent and censor names we've never had to censor before.

"You can't actually agree to this." She says this as a statement, not a question.

"I wanted to talk to you first," I say. I don't like making decisions in a vacuum.

In the last few weeks, this *ESPN* deal has gotten worse and worse.

"Listen, the fact that they'd censor my name is a huge red flag," she says. In my mind, part of it has hinged on whether or not Victoria qualified for the final day of game play, which they have. But I see how it's actually a bright red flag that *ESPN* feels squeamish about references to anything non-hetero.

"And if not me," Bicepsual adds, "it would've just been someone else's name they tried to censor for ridiculous reasons. Either way, it's shit." I think of the list in red and know she's absolutely correct. One of the other names they'd asked about is Rose City's Frisky Biscuits, which isn't even close to being inappropriate. It all feels like a control mechanism more than an FCC requirement.

Meeting Bicepsual's eyes again, I realize none of this means anything if it's not for the skaters, for the community. For us. There's no mention of *ESPN* in *by the skaters, for the skaters.* Or, the more modern, equitable take, *by the community, for the community.*

"You're right. I think we should tell them to go to hell." I throw my hands up, angry. "Fuck them. You're right. We spent forty thousand dollars of the WFTDA's money on this broadcast. That's a lot of fucking money. That's more money than most of us make in a year. But for them to dick us around like this, fuck it. What's it worth to show something that's not really us?"

I think of my son and his fellow junior skaters. What would I want them to take from all of this? That your identity is negotiable? That you compromise who you are?

"Totally my point," Bicepsual says.

A pang stabs at my heart as I see clearly how I've led us here. I am still painfully learning how to push back against male-dominated systems, to claim my value. To be a team player and also stand up for myself. This pang in my chest explodes as I open my mouth again.

"Fuck it," I say. "Fuck *ESPN*."

"Yeah?"

"Yeah. Go tell your team, and I'll talk to the officials. Maybe we can broadcast the show after the fact on a network that'll actually appreciate us."

What is the soul of a sport worth? Or the soul of the people who lead it? Our roller derby broadcast season brings in close to $100,000 dollars in profit, when all is said and done. It pays my $60,000 a year salary and puts money back into the sport. Into education and competition. And in that Philadelphia arena basement, I determine easily that I'd rather give up on ESPN than sacrifice who we are.

In the film business, we used to call this *killing your babies*— or, ridding ourselves of something sparkly that we loved for the benefit of the whole product. Editors and directors often cut some of their favorite shots and scenes from films and television shows, in order to tell a better story. Leaving the *ESPN* show on the cutting room floor was a devastating but necessary part of embracing who roller derby most authentically is.

"Derby is a grassroots skater owned and operated

organization," says Jane McManus, "And that was central to the ethos. This is why there's a trans inclusion policy and not an *exclusion* policy. But you were working in a media environment that did not take you seriously. And that wasn't just *ESPN*, because *ESPN* looked your way for a minute. But *Fox Sports* didn't look your way. *Bleacher Report* didn't look your way."

And that's what was gutting about it. Media coverage we got was either slutshaming us, making us out to be Wingettes, or asking us for compromises we shouldn't have had to make. For a moment, I thought *ESPN* had finally gotten us.

"Those letters meant something, *ESPN*," shares Stefanie Madison, former head of WFTDA Talent Management. "We showed that we're good enough to be on that stage—with our own announcers, our camera angles, our skaters and officials, and were just as good as the people I grew up watching on that network."

I shared our collective disappointment with the *ESPN* program manager in an email.

If there is an FCC obscenity violation in place, the WFTDA is 100% committed to abiding by those regulations and guidelines. However, the WFTDA feels that banning the use of "Bicepsual" is discriminatory in its approach to our LGBTQ community members. If the assumption on behalf of the network is that "bisexual" is an indecent term, we disagree, and find this to be absolutely counter to everything we stand for.

Writing these words to the program manager at *ESPN*, I knew full well I was probably burning this bridge. Severing a connection I'd spent years trying to build. Most broadcasters and producers in sports would focus their life's work on trying to cultivate great relationships with the likes of *ESPN*. But when I sat with what they asked from us, the cost was too high.

I appreciate everything you do and continue to do for the WFTDA and for roller derby as a sport. If the network decides not to run our show for the use of "Bicepsual," we will be disappointed, but mostly because of the missed opportunity that you have as a network, to make sports a more inclusive place for all viewers and athletes. We leave it in your hands to decide whether you'd like to pursue running this, knowing that perhaps the network is not as inclusive as we'd like it to be just yet.

"We're not broadcasting on *ESPN2* this weekend," I say, looking around at a bevy of quizzical faces. On Saturday, I stand in the middle of a circle during halftime, with all of the captains, plus all of the officials for the game, the head officials for the tournament, and the head announcer. "And we're tentative for *ESPN3*. We were hoping to be able to push out live television tomorrow, but that changed."

"Couldn't get the teams to agree to name changes?" One of the officials asks.

"No," I say. "We shouldn't have to change names." Someone coughs, and all of the eyes remain open, alert, waiting for my rationale. "I just talked to the Board. You can thank Bicepsual from Victoria, who very persuasively reminded me that this is our fucking game, and we shouldn't have to change it for anybody."

"Yeah it is," one of the captains says. It reminds me of

Hydra's words from our interview years ago. *I hope the skaters always have a say.*

"This is our sport," I say. "We get to say whose name is appropriate and inappropriate. If the biggest sports network in the world can't handle it, fuck 'em. We'll do it our way."

Every single face in the group nods back at me in agreement.

"Bring it in," I say, and the group of a dozen or so pulls in, shoulder to shoulder. "Everyone's name stays, officials, announcers, and skaters. We're doing this our way, and we're doing it together. Okay?"

"Fuck yes," an official says, nodding.

"Hands in," I say, putting my hand in the center of the circle. I catch the head official laughing as he puts his hand in. "Fuck *ESPN* on three," I say. "One, two, three."

"*Fuck ESPN.*" Our rallying cry is failure, only I don't know yet how deep that truth will cut.

Illustration by Sandra Frame,
a.k.a. Tara Armov.

cutting the track

verb

---

when a skater is blocked over the inside or outside track boundary line and re-enters in front of the skater who forced them out of bounds; a penalty.

CHAPTER 31:

Back to the Beginning

Saturday Night. November, 2017. Philadelphia, Pennsylvania.

"We'll be back after the half in this Gotham, Rose City game," I say, leading us into a halftime break for commercials. It's after nine p.m., and the crowd in the arena buzzes below. Taking off my headset and plopping it on the table in front of me, I turn back to my colleagues. Our producer leans towards me, rubbing his gray sideburns with a pen.

"That'll need an apology," my producer says.

"Yeah," my co-announcer agrees. "That wasn't the smoothest way to say things, H."

"What did I say?" I rub my eyes. I honestly don't know. Then my producer spells it out.

"You said, 'one of these teams will go home a winner, and one of these teams will go home in a *'trail of tears,'*" my producer says. It's his job to track information for the game, including the kind of bullshit I just said.

"Oh, fuck," I groan. I'd barely finished licking my wounds from *ESPN*. Now this. I replay the call in my head, remember watching Gotham skate off the track, the stats flashing on the screen. "I was reaching for like… three words. *A fireball of despair. A blaze of glory.* Fuck. Not that." A new feeling I have is unmistakable. It's wringing at my stomach, tightening around my esophagus. It's terrible, this feeling: shame. That I am tired doesn't excuse anything. It only amplifies it.

My producer has a laptop open on the announcer's table in front of us. Amid the headset cables and wires, he has social media open and a growing handful of people have started to weigh in on my comment on Twitter. He sighs, "It was definitely… noticed."

Really, Double H? Making fun of genocide? #Talk2WFTDA
What does that even mean? Explain for us Europeans.
She shouldn't be on a mic. Unacceptable. #Talk2WFTDA

I feel sick to my stomach.

"Thirty seconds," our producer says. Taking a deep breath, I put my headset on, wrapping my head around the crushing idiocy that came out of my own mouth.

"One team will go on to compete for the Hydra, and one will go home in a *trail of tears.*" After I uttered this sentence, I sat with it. Somewhere between wanting to be witty and just being lazy, I'd ended up saying something totally offensive. We'd come a long way from Hookers jokes and Hitler-themed names in roller derby. We'd fought for inclusion—I'd fought for inclusion. In any other sport in the world, my comments might have been questioned, then brushed aside. But in roller derby, the community drives our values.

"A lot of the derby community were calling on us to call

you in," says April Fournier, a.k.a. Jumpy McGee, Team Indigenous co-founder, speaking about that day at the 2017 Championships. "I was just getting pinged on Twitter."

Fournier had played roller derby for over a decade at the time. A Navajo educator with Native Organizers Alliance and co-founder of the borderless global collective, Team Indigenous, Fournier is also a mother of four. She and I were both raised in New England, a part of the country steeped in the roots of colonization. In my own eighties childhood, teachers skimmed past the Trail of Tears, the Wampanoag, and the word "genocide" altogether. I knew about these things and I knew they weren't funny. I certainly wasn't thinking about colonizers and genocide when I put those three words together during a roller derby broadcast. And really, that is a great example of white folks like me not thinking before they speak and gravitating toward dated, white supremacy-based references for humor.

That same colonialism-based language needs a lot of undoing in team names and mascots, as well. For example, only in 2018 did Cleveland's baseball team finally agree to stop using their degrading Chief Wahoo[52] logo, featuring a smiling Indigenous caricature. The logo, an article from *The Wrap* reports, "has been in use by the former Cleveland Indians since 1947, but in recent years both the logo and the team's name have been criticized as racist. In 2000, the Penobscot Indian Nation formally asked the team to ditch the logo."

In the NFL, the Washington Commanders also relented by eliminating not only their logos, but their name—before even having a suitable replacement name chosen. The "Washington

Football Team" name debuted in 2020.[53]

In roller derby, we gave a shit about racism and colonization. Or, if community members couldn't wrap their heads around that, at least they understood that at some point, we've all been *othered*. Roller derby is a collective of trans women, cisgender women, nonbinary humans. At some point or other, most of us here have been marginalized, at least in some capacity. And those feelings aren't good.

"One of my biggest frustrations," says Fournier, "still, is that... over and over again, it falls to the community that is harmed to be the educators, to step in and say, 'This is a learning moment for everyone.'" April was the first person to reach out directly to me after my comments. One of the members of Team Indigenous even counseled me on writing my public apology. I noted that others in the community—lots of white folks—were silent. Probably because they didn't know what to say.

"In those learning moments, you have very upper level teams with giant platforms," Fournier adds, "all-star skaters are often radio silent when any of these issues happen. I don't know if it's because, 'Oh, I don't want to get political.' People who hold those positions don't take that risk, and it still falls to the community that was harmed."

When someone tells you that you've harmed them, is your first instinct to protect your ego or put yourself in the shoes of the folks you've harmed? I admit, I sucked at this. Yet, this was the work roller derby demanded of me—difficult, uncomfortable, necessary.

What I knew almost immediately was that there was no

magic bullet to fix this. That I would try to rebuild trust by listening, getting to work, and putting the community's needs ahead of my own. This moment—this mistake—didn't just change how I speak. It changed how I listen.

"I wanted to take a moment today to apologize for a callous and insensitive comment I made on last night's broadcast." I say these words into the camera before we start our final day of Championships in Philadelphia. I'm feeling into the edges of what it means to carry privilege and I'm not liking it.

"Please always let me know where I can support you better, be a better ally, and work hard to earn back your trust when I have let you down," I finish. Though it's not anyone else's responsibility to teach me how to rebuild that trust. The WFTDA social media volunteer who's recording me gives a sympathetic smile as she puts the camera down, ending the live feed. I thank her and the Board members in the room. Retreating to a vacant locker room, I sit, reading yet more comments on social media.

Crocodile tears, Double H.

This is the most fake, insincere apology I've ever heard.

Are we really going to believe this trash human?

In roller derby, we train to fall and get back up. We learn how to hit the ground, slide, pull ourselves up to standing again—I teach my son this all the time. And other children who count on me as a role model. But there's no training for a fall like this when the impact is emotional.

You okay, Hymen? Sitting in the locker room, I get a text

from The Cyclone. One of the few people who still call me that—*Hymen. Hymen Heaven.* What would she think of this?

After staring at the screen for a few seconds, I respond. *I will be.*

I know you. I know your heart.

I say nothing.

This wasn't a back block or other penalty I could serve. This was me, falling flat on my face in full view of the community that taught me how to get back up. Only, in that moment, I wasn't sure if I could.

A bright spot: 2017 Champs had more women on the mic than any previous Championship. Photo credit: Emily Mills.

halftime speech

noun

---

the type of pep talk a coach is expected to give a team halfway through the game, especially if the team is losing.

CHAPTER 32:

Halftime

Winter, 2018. Philadelphia, Pennsylvania.

It's a gray mid-Winter morning in Manchester. I'm in the UK for the Roller Derby World Cup, a four-day tournament event that draws teams from around the world. An event outside the WFTDA, but is good for gameplay—and great for roller derby.

A blue and yellow and white shirt ahead of me says, "*Roller derby saved my soul*" in Greek. I can tell because, as the person turns, the phrasing is duplicated in English. It hits me how many souls have been saved by this sport. Or, at least, entrusted to it. How many of us found our way here, like I did. Messy, imperfect. I still think about the harm I caused in November every day. How I'm not here to talk, I'm here to listen.

This is the first time I'm stepping out again in public, to be seen as the interim Executive Director of the WFTDA. To say I'm nervous about this is an understatement. Peering up from my phone for a moment, I catch a group of officials a few yards away; one of them catches my eye, then whispers to the others. I make small fists in my gloves to distract myself.

I turn back to my phone. Deep down, I wonder if *ESPN* did this intentionally, if the sports network created a flop with our content on purpose so they could keep any future deals more advantageous to them. Keep us humble and wanting to chase after them. *Keep us in our place. With cornhole.*

I don't have time to think about it as the doors ahead open with the raucous sounds of "Tubthumping" by Chumbawamba. A man with a Mancunian twinge calls out into the morning. "Those with tickets, queue at the left, those needing to buy tickets, queue to the right, please."

I unfold my paper ticket and walk into the venue portal at the Roller Derby World Cup, a gigantic venue with a handful of columns and tens of thousands of square feet with gleaming concrete floors.

"Fuck, I want to skate on this," I whisper, marveling at the surface. Beyond the ticketing tables, four full oval tracks are laid out in a four-square pattern. Zig-zagging around the venue are handfuls of skaters on and off skates, officials, announcers, spectators, meandering in as everyone prepares for the day's first handful of games.

Directly in front of the entrance, a whole village of booths and locker rooms spread out in squares all around the facility. Tables sell T-shirts and pins, buttons and pennants of all different colors, shapes and sizes. Manufacturers and clothing sellers line tiny streets with all kinds of wares to sell. A giant paper bracket stuck to the wall at the left of the entrance maps out the games for the day, with almost forty teams from around the globe.

One of them, Team Indigenous Roller Derby, pulls athletes from all over the world, a borderless team, like Jewish Roller Derby. Teams without borders, formed through shared identity rather than geography. A rejection of colonial frameworks that I—awkward and still learning—am suddenly, profoundly grateful for.

So, this is roller derby, I think. The hair on the back of my arms tingles as I realize how great all of this is, how important it is. How it's grown, wild and organically. And fuck, I'm still smitten. After all of these years.

"I wanted a sport where everyone could be themselves," shares Amy Sherman, a.k.a. Electra Blu, a godmother, a founder of flat track roller derby. "We used to sew our own stuff on our uniforms, you know? I miss that."

Her point is well taken. When the founding mothers—the godmothers—of the sport of flat track roller derby set out to build something, there were no role models for what they were building. They weren't thinking about gender expansiveness or equity or change management. They weren't sure where they were headed, where any of this was truly leading. What they had in mind wasn't so much a destination as it was a feeling, a culture. And it was fun.

"As it hyper-focused on the sport, and not worrying about the spectacle," says Corndog, Joshua Thompson, formerly of Gotham, "the crowds became friends and family, and tournaments just turned into conventions… But we thought we were doing the right thing. What we didn't know was what the cost would be."

And in steering us toward so-called legitimacy, I'd side-stepped what had made us magnetic in the first place: we weren't made for onlookers, we were made for each other.

"If a brand or a social media influencer could get the sort of cult-like engagement that roller derby has, it would be over. Destination, the moon," says former Executive Director, Cassie Haynes. "Yet roller derby was never meant to be a publicly consumed sport."

And this, as I was learning, was also never a weakness but a superpower. We were never built to play by anyone else's rules. Now, finally, I was starting to see what playing by our own rules could look like.

Plastik Patrik, Catherine BeatHer Bonez,
and Double H at Roller Derby World Cup
in Manchester.
Photo credit: Paul Robertson/Preflash Gordon.

the long game

noun

---

a strategy of playing roller derby with the goal of wearing down your opponent over time, knowing statistically you're scoring more points overall.

CHAPTER 33:

Playing the Long Game

Summer, 2018. Philadelphia, Pennsylvania.

For the second year in a row, ESPN will suspend regularly scheduled programming on one of its networks to bring fans the finest in seldom-seen sports from around the globe.

Almost a year after cancelling our broadcast, *ESPN: The Ocho* website features a variety of sports on it—all of them parody sports. A joke website based on the gag network created for the comedy film *Dodgeball*. On *The Ocho* landing page, folks are boxing with KFC fast food buckets on their heads, then sitting down to play chess. Chess boxing. And there, next to them, is roller derby.

Not just any roller derby, but the 2017 WFTDA Championship game, the one we'd poured our money, sweat, and soul into. The greatest story never sold.

"Oh no they fucking didn'-," I mutter as I read the website over. I can't imagine they'd be stupid enough to run this on *The Ocho*, a gag site. Not after all they put us through. Not after inviting us to pay $40,000 out of our own pockets to produce a show they booted off live television. The entire vibe on the website positions these as quirky spectacles. Not niche sports with unique value, but as novelty acts for "24 hours of fun."

In this moment, I feel what it means to be reduced to a farce. A joke. Either *ESPN* doesn't get how this lands, or they do and they just don't care. Neither of these options sit well with me. I remember how *ESPN's* producer had asked if roller derby was real. Guess we got our answer. To them, we were clearly never real enough to invest in. And it was time for me to tell them.

Jane McManus tells part of this story in her 2025 book, *The Fast Track: Inside the Surging Business of Women's Sports* (Temple Press). "(T)he network decided to put the event on its gimmicky day broadcasting as *The Ocho*, a reference to a running joke in the movie *Dodgeball*. The WFTDA is an organization made up of the women who play, and many didn't want their premiere showcase of skill and strategy to be a punchline."

After seeing *The Ocho*, I penned an open letter to *ESPN*[54] that the WFTDA posted online.

Your network basically said they were canceling a women's sport from live broadcast because of the actions of a handful of sexist men. Let that sink in, and you may understand why I needed to write this letter...

As a person with a certain amount of power or privilege who's made mistakes, I know you don't always see the error of your ways. I'm willing to give network executives the benefit of the doubt. Yet, with *ESPN*, it just felt like they didn't necessarily give a fuck about us. And that stung.

ESPN made it obvious that the WFTDA was an uncomfortable reach for them. During the course of our conversations, there was increased scrutiny and focus on the names of skaters and officials… In light of this history, I hope you can understand why it is upsetting to the roller derby community to see future airings of our content being promoted with the use of phrases like "barely a sport," images of clumsy pseudo-athletes with chicken buckets on their heads, and that list our sport alongside activities such as wife-carrying, eating contests, and mascot challenges.

…I still stand by the words I wrote to you last November: If you're unhappy with our show… we will be disappointed, but mostly because of the missed opportunity that you have as a network, to make sports a more inclusive place for all viewers and athletes. Do better. #DoBetterESPN.

I ended my *ESPN* letter with a hashtag, knowing it'd be posted online—*#DoBetterESPN*. I wasn't sure what it would bring the WFTDA, or me, as an Executive Director. But I didn't give a fuck about that. As it turned out, neither did roller derby.

I'm proud to skate with this organization!
This is my sport, my community. #Talk2WFTDA
Double H didn't come here to fuck spiders!

One of the comments on social media days later from an Australian skater was my favorite. The term, *didn't come to fuck spiders*, is a cheeky Australian way of saying someone's not messing around. And it's true, with *ESPN*, there were no spiders to be fucked in my estimation. Not when roller derby's soul was on the line.

At the end of the day, all of this matters to me because people just want to play roller derby. Or officiate, or announce, or DJ, or take photographs. It's an exhilarating, kick-ass community with room for innovation and invention. I tried to honor that every day of the year as Interim Executive Director, and later my subsequent three years as permanent Executive Director. Even as I came shoulder-to-shoulder with the greatest opponent I've ever faced on or off the track—mother nature, herself.

England vs. Mexico, Roller Derby World Cup
in Manchester, 2018.
Photo credit: Paul Robertson/Preflash Gordon.

turn stop

noun

---

a type of stop where the skater turns around, landing on toe stops or otherwise, to change direction, halting their speed and redirecting them.

CHAPTER 34:

Shut It Down

March, 2020. Outside of Baltimore, Maryland.

"Vanstone, hold her!" one of my teammates hollers from across the track. After almost fifteen years in the sport, I'm back to using my last name. I'm also chest-to-chest with my opposing jammer—not an ideal position for any blocker to be. Solo blocking, open and exposed.

It's early March 2020 and my Philly B-Team is taking on Charm City's All Stars. I feel my fellow blocker touch my back, which means it's time to flip around and grab the jammer with my booty. As I do, the jammer makes a break for it. My teammate catches her with an outside hip. Together, we recapture her and drive her laterally across the track towards the outside line.

"Holding," I hear my teammate grunt. I flip to brace her.

Charm City's jammer is short and muscular, attempting to break past us. As the brace, I keep my teammate's hip plastered to the jammer, so that whatever direction she turns, my blocker can stay on her. I readjust to stay in front of it all.

"You got her," I say softly. "Just stay low." The other part of bracing is keeping your fellow blockers calm. Charm's jammer looks up at the jam clock and groans. She brings her hands to her hips, calling off the jam. As the whistle blows, my team-mate nods.

"That was great," she pants. We high-five as we exit the track.

We're at least fifty points behind Baltimore. Every jam is a new jam. I don't know this will be the last roller derby game I'll ever formally play in my life. The last high-fives, the last derby sweat. And perhaps it's better that way. I'm not sure I would have done anything differently, had I known otherwise. Especially if the goal of roller derby—of any sport—is to do your best in every single time you step out onto the track. Whether you know it's your last time or not.

In April 2020, I was no longer just interim, I was the Executive Director of a global amateur sport during a once-in-a-century pandemic. Forty thousand athletes. Four hundred fifty-six clubs. Thirty-three countries. All of them waiting for me to tell them what to do. In turn, I waited on the U.S. federal government—or, any federal government—to give me recommendations for amateur sports communities. A wait that turned into a guessing game.

Each state, each city, each sport, was left to solve these problems on their own. The NBA and MLB dumped money into frequent testing and isolated competition. The NBA, in particular, developed competition bubbles[55] to keep players quarantined and still have a basketball season. It involved assuming that every player could avoid COVID—a disease whose death toll was mounting.

Roller derby was not that. We were a community built on a DIY culture, with little money but lots of room for innovation. One of my biggest frustrations with the Trump administration was the lack of knowledge being shared, which is what roller derby often excelled at. I kept coming back to a burning question: What rate of COVID-19 infection was an acceptable amount of cases for us to consider playing a contact sport? Even asking that felt surreal. But this was the job now.

I wasn't a scientist. I was a filmmaker-turned-sports executive. Only, yet again, I knew if the world wasn't going to build a system that incorporated roller derby, we were going to have to do it ourselves. Writing complex, inclusive policy is what roller derby lives by. I wasn't afraid to do it again.

Both on social media and in our internal forums, I put out the call for frontline workers and medical professionals in the community. An epidemiologist, an anesthesiologist, a trauma physician, a registered nurse, and a handful of other volunteers joined me in creating our own public health guidelines.

We started with the number of COVID-19 cases being reported each week. Even though every city shared data differently, the data itself was mostly uniform. Since the Center for Disease Control[56] was using fifty cases per 100,000 as its baseline metric for dropping quarantines, we used this number to create a ladder.

Clubs would need to watch for these levels to determine when they could step on the ladder, or restart skating. I worked with the team and staff to develop guidelines that graduated clubs from skating to contact, using this ladder and a simple spreadsheet calculator to track their cases—our *Roller Derby Return to Play Guidelines.*[57]

And it didn't go unnoticed.

"Leave it to a women's sports organization to put together a quite reasonable return plan," says Emory University epidemiologist Zachary Binney in a June 2020 *WIRED*[58] magazine article. Professor Binney, a sports fan, became an unwitting ally to flat track roller derby with his take. "The section spelling out the policy on spectators is so good, it almost made me cry."

"The roller derby guidelines put community and player health ahead of the need to keep the game going for the sake of eager fans," *WIRED* reported—or, what roller derby was calling putting *lives before laces.* "Meanwhile, in other sports, efforts to resume play continue even as cases turn up among players."

The NBA had bubbles. The MLB had rapid testing and private jets. Roller derby had the internet, volunteers, and Excel formulas. Other sports moved forward with contact, despite the risks, while our skater-forward Return to Play Guidelines were downloaded by Harvard TH Chan School of Public Health, Ontario Health, the Minnesota Air National Guard, and more.

When roller derby was forced to make decisions about how to handle COVID, we didn't know about "long" COVID—but we erred on the side that it had shitty consequences, no matter what. So our goal was to avoid transmission altogether.

We effectively shut down the sport, and it wasn't without a lot of pushback.

#LetUsSkate WFTDA!
Our city's roller derby team is going to fold because you won't let us play.
How dare you tell us what to do with our bodies, you hypocrites.

As Executive Director, I responded with the same positive, outward-facing message—that we are keeping the community at the forefront, that we're saving lives. Yet I knew there were serious business implications to this decision, both for the mother organization, and for roller derby's clubs.

"I've been in derby for twenty years," says Nili Goldfarb, a.k.a. Isabelle Ringer, owner of San Diego Derby United and Ringer's Rink. After getting kicked out of their warehouse in 2019, San Diego's new facility opened just days before COVID-19 shut it down. "One minute we were hugging, cutting the red ribbon. The next week, we had to shut it all down."

Kim Stegeman, a.k.a. Rocket Mean, Executive Director of Rose City Rollers, concurs. "I white knuckled that shit," she says of managing her organization through COVID. She adds, "I pulled a train up a hill—and people either loved me or hated me for it."

But this is the work roller derby, and other women-led spaces, are asked to do: innovate in the face of uncertainty. Because we put public health above profit, press coverage on our plan was overwhelmingly positive, including an October 2020 segment of *Full Frontal with Samantha Bee*, who applauded our choices. "There's one sport that's reopening the right way," says Samantha Bee, "and America can learn a lot from it."

Whether or not America ever wants to learn anything from

roller derby is another story. Yet our plan worked. By 2021, roller derby came through the other side of the COVID-19 pandemic with 60% of our staff and Board, and 375 remaining clubs. And not a single reported death from COVID-19—zero.

Zero deaths. Zero lives lost to roller derby. Including men and juniors. It's a number that proves roller derby may not be poised to save any souls. But it sure as fuck is ready to save lives.

Minnesota Roller Derby
returning from COVID-19.
Photo credit: Paul Robertson/Preflash Gordon.

star pass

noun

---

when a jammer is unable to break free from the pack and passes the helmet cover to her pivot, making the pivot the team's new jammer in that jam.

CHAPTER 35:

Don't Let Them Eat the Baby

Fall, 2021. Philadelphia, Pennsylvania.

Real. Strong. Athletic. Revolutionary.

Roller derby is all of these things. And at the end of 2021, it was also still very much alive. That November, I quietly stepped down as WFTDA's Executive Director, moving over to run the for-profit subsidiary, the insurance division, to rebuild revenue. I say *quietly* because there really is no playbook for how to handle a pandemic as a leader. And after doing everything I could to hold the community together until COVID vaccines arrived, I was tired.

"COVID was a tough time and it seems like a lot of leagues haven't recovered from that period," says Jennifer Wilson, a.k.a. Hydra—godmother of the sport. "But derby made it to the other side, which is inspiring and shows great resilience."

My four years running the sport were some of the hardest, most grueling, and most rewarding moments of my life. At least, to date. Resilience is one of the biggest gifts I carry with me from my time in roller derby—the ability to get back up, no matter what. That, and a deep sense of knowing myself.

Having forty thousand lives in your hands shows you who you really are. There's no unseeing the compassion that's needed, no unfeeling the fear and uncertainty.

Still, no one told me how high the cost of cultivating the gift of resilience would be. I lost friends, colleagues, board members, volunteers, staff members, budgetary funds—yet, oddly, I found me. The real me. The me who fucked up royally and still woke up every day thinking, *I have to keep trying*. The me who really believes every jam is a new jam because she has to.

As a skater, official, announcer, broadcaster, and finally, leader, I wanted to leave the sport having accomplished something—to win back trust, to prepare roller derby for a whole new future. But sometimes, the best thing you can do as a leader is be a relief jammer. A placeholder. A space-taker. I didn't realize I was taking this space so the rest of the world could catch up.

Roller derby is so far ahead of its time, especially now. Waking up every day to a federal administration that finds new ways to take rights away from Americans tells me something critical. That the work this world needs is the work roller derby's been doing all along: deep reflection on community values. Structural changes based on those needs. Making space for new ideas. It's the greatest story never sold for a reason: maybe the world just isn't ready for that yet.

"There's nothing like roller derby," says Jocelyn Jenik, a.k.a. the Cycrone, who's also since retired from the sport. "I can never recreate it. I can have new relationships, but no one will ever replace the relationship I had with all of you."

These relationships mean everything. The sport is intense, demanding, outspoken, loving, and difficult. It is not for the faint of heart. Our whole lives, women—cisgender, trangender, and fluid—have been told we need to be nurturing. To be nice, to be fair. To be meek, to be protected. The fact that roller derby gives us the glimmer of being able to be all of those things, yet strong and fierce at the same time isn't a vulnerability, it's an asset.

Whether anyone else in mainstream sports or federal governments or the media can see that, I now know, is irrelevant.

Stefanie Madison, former broadcaster and head of WFTDA Talent Management, agrees. "I would love for us to still be on *ESPN* and be part of the national conversation but we're just not and it happens. We took our best swing and it didn't work. But we still fucking swung."

The fact that we got so far, that roller derby made it back to television, that we took a good look at equity, that we led the way for other sports during a global pandemic—and as authentically *us*. Flaws and all. What other sports can say that? Heck, what other organization outside of sports can?

We had the greatest sports story ever told but chose to give it up to focus on community. And that's how we survived. It's how I, personally, survived. This is the work of feminism moving forward—*the real work*. To persist. To remain vital and present in the moment, no matter how much it hurts, how much people push back, or how often you fall.

And falling. Well, I seem to have a talent for that. My saving grace has actually been to do it all so publicly. Not as a warning to others, but as a lesson. Especially to younger generations, both in and outside of roller derby. Gen Zs and Gen Alpha kids who are going to need grit and tenacity to slog through cultural bullshit. They'll need grace, wit, and humor. They'll need softness and smarts and toughness. And above all, they're going to need *Believance*.

"Coulda used you for a star pass, Catman."

A short, blonde skater is giving my son some feedback. I'm coaching Philly Roller Derby's junior B-Team, The Brawlstars, a team that includes boys and girls, as well as genderqueer, genderfluid, and nonbinary kids. All on the same teams— what the rest of the world might refer to as co-ed, part of Jerry Seltzer's original vision.

"Catman?" I ask my son. "Did you hear your teammate? You're the pivot, yeah?" I tap his helmet to remind him he has the pivot cover on. As the pivot, he's the only one who can take the star if the jammer gets trapped. And she did. Twice. Now, the score is nearly tied at the half.

"Oh," he says, feeling the top of his helmet. "Right, sorry."

"Is roller derby an individual sport?"

A handful of heads shake back and forth. "No," a few of them grumble. My other coach adds a few words about blocking and getting lower. And urgency, which makes me smile, remembering Holden Killfield's critical lessons.

"Bring it in," I say, waving my hand. The Brawlstars comply, forming a loose, heavily breathing little circle around me. I scan their tiny, dewy faces.

"Alright, everyone yell 'Brawlstars' on three. Ready? One,

two, three…"

"*Brawlstars!*" they holler in unison, lifting their small, wrist-guard-covered hands.

"Catman, keep the pivot cap on," my fellow coach says, tapping his head as we prepare to go into the second period. She looks down at a paper with the roster and lineups.

"Me?" he asks. "I thought I messed it up?"

"Yes, you," she says, "but you're going to do it right this time, right?" She adjusts the pivot cap on his head and he smooths it to ensure it's on tight.

"Right," he says. Still, the look on his face tells me he's uncertain. He lets out a large sigh. I know exactly how he feels—I've been here before. Just trying to not fuck up.

"*Five seconds!*" yells a non-skating official, a woman in a black-and-white striped jersey in the center of the track. The opposing junior jammer, a tiny skater with red hair, sets up near the inside line. My own jammer flips her two blonde braids over each shoulder, then drifts near the outside. Crouching into position, on the sidelines, I watch and wait.

The whistle blows to start the jam. Journey's "Don't Stop Believin'" strums in the background.

Our Brawlstars jammer accelerates into Jersey's wall. Immediately, she's stuck behind a wall of short bodies. Looking over to her opponent on the inside line, our jammer hesitates. Then, instead of attacking the wall, she turns to hit her opponent to the inside, knocking her out of bounds.

"What is she doing?" My fellow coach asks.

"I dunno," I mumble. Without warning, our jammer starts to skate clockwise, in the non-derby direction. It's a tactic I haven't seen on a track for over a decade. Our skater is trying to get the fellow jammer to follow her all the way around the track so our blockers can trap her. The other team's jammer looks at her bench. I hear her coaches hollering. *"No! Don't let them eat the baby!"*

"Oh my god!" I scream. "Yes! Eat the baby! Eat the baby!"

"We haven't practiced this!" my fellow coach yells.

I guffaw, incredulous. These kids are executing a strategy that almost dates back to the year I walked into a skate rink in Camden, New Jersey. And we didn't teach them this. Our mini jammer plods all the way backwards around the track, drawing her opposing jammer back to where the pack is starting—doing a full lap in reverse. Our blockers look confused.

I yell to them. "Get up and move in front of her!" I point, instructing them to capture the opposing jammer, as the Broad Street Butchers and Heavy Metal Hookers once did. "Go trap her." I can't stop grinning. "We're gonna eat the baby."

My son nods, complying. He and his three fellow blockers race to get in front of the opposing jammer. They succeed. I plant my hands on my head in disbelief and turn to my fellow coach. *"Our babies just ate the baby!"*

My fellow coach cackles. "Where the hell did they learn that?"

"From us," I laugh.

But Philly's jammer gets hung up in the pack again herself, waiting for our blockers to move. Like we taught her, she pulls the fabric star from her head. *Time for a star pass.*

"Catman!" I yell. My son turns his head and looks behind to see his jammer, arm outstretched. Angling his left arm back, he does as he's been taught—he grabs the helmet cover with the star and runs. On skates. He's not lead jammer, but now he can score points.

"I can't believe our babies ate the baby," I say, over and over.

"Star pass to Philly's pivot, Catman," I hear the announcer's voice echoing across the rink and I'm jumping up and down.

"Go, Catman, go!" I hear my own voice. This time, I'm rooting for a team I'm not playing on, but one I'm managing. One I'm teaching to be way better than I've ever been at roller derby—or, at anything else, really. And they've got their own unique surprises.

I watch my son's cherubic face huffing and puffing as he rounds turn three and back to the pack. He skates faster. By some miracle, Jersey is still fixated on freeing their jammer on the inside of the track. Catman aims for the outside line and speeds up to outrun an incoming blocker. Sailing around her, he clears the pack with twenty seconds left in the jam.

"Five points, Philly!" the announcer howls.

"Go, go, go," my other coach waves him on and he nods, pushing around the track one more time to try to score points. Wiping the sweat from his eyes, my son barrels towards the pack one more time. As he approaches the wall, he executes a spin move, looping past an opponent by skating sideways. Just like on *SportsCenter*.

"Holy shit," the other coach says. "We're doing it." She grabs my shoulder.

My heart soars. Higher and fuller than it's ever done when I've done any of this for myself. And I understand now that lifting others up is the greatest gift a sport can give. It's a high

I didn't expect. And it's glorious.

Whether you're smart or weird or different, that's okay. All roller derby asks of you is your best. If you can muster that, if you can give everything you can possibly give—if you can leave it all on the track—you've been successful.

As the jam comes to a conclusion and I watch my kid high five his teammates, our bench floods with smiles and laughter. The opposing team takes a time out, and I know now, the real joy here isn't winning. It's discovering who we are, moment by moment.

The lesson—the *real* one—was never: *Can roller derby save your soul?* It's... can *you*?

ACKNOWLEDGMENTS

Writing a book is a team sport, and there are so many team members to thank for their encouragement and cheerleading along the way.

First, I need to thank my agent Amy Giuffrida and Belcastro Agency for believing in this book. Without Amy, in fact, this book might not exist. When I walked into a writer's conference in 2023, she looked me in the eye and said, "I love the concept, now go write it." So I did. Which brings me to Michelle Kicherer.

Michelle, who took me in as a meek, unseasoned memoir writer and held my hand as I became an author. Michelle believed in this book, and in this story, enough to be my writing coach through several drafts. I'm so grateful to Michelle and the team at Banana Pitch Press for giving this book a good home! Special thanks to Gwen Schulte at GRS Editorial for your design and editing work, and Chris Hendrix for your expertise in all things Kickstarter. More good things to come!

Next, in my time with roller derby, there have been so many wonderful humans to thank, including my OG Philly Roller Derby friends, Jon Goff, Kellie Goldberg, Jocelyn Jenik, Rich

Shriver, Jon Dilks, Elaine Kilmartin, Kristen Hermann, Kevin and Melissa Walter, Maureen Stubbs, Mishel Castro, Kristi DellaBadia, Mary Dunham, Michael and Mandy Wehrman, Ivanna Rock, and more. Oh, and to Dee Thurner and Somerset Splits, my Heavy Metal Hookers, Broad Street Butchers, and Philthy Britches, I'll love you forever!

I'd also love to thank my voices of reason, my fellow roller derby announcers, including John and Tavanna Porter, Mike Chexx, Sandra Frame, Amy Sherman, Randy Hughes, Joshua Thompson, Nami Bigos, Lauren Bishop, Anthony Mansfield, Ryan Caesar, Jake Merriman, Etienne LaFond, Alicia Greene, Melissa Chamberlain, Adam Kenyon, Andrew Wencer, Tracy Williams, Ashlie Atkinson, Megan Dahl, Steve Arkle, Plastik Patrik, Jeff O'Neill, Valphonse Capone, Ryan Parker, Dan Mossman, Dave Miller, Chip Wright, Ryan Will, and so many more.

WFTDA.tv truly took a village to create, and folks like Dr. Michelle Cartier, Victoria Gonzalez, Kevin Borke, Benjamin Doyle, Derek Willis, Kimberly Gehl, and so many more created outstanding content alongside me and Blaze Streaming Media's Joe Christensen. And to Ray Colaiacovo and his crew, and Jason Weber at NFL Films for always seeing the vision. Thank you all for believing in our work together! I miss you all so much!

WFTDA Marketing and Volunteers helped keep us promoted, like Leanne Terpak, Courtney Caballero, Rachel Johnston, Erin McCargar, Kali Schumitz, Dedi Hubbard, Brian Gadell, Mike Fiedler, and so many others. The WFTDA Staff, of course, has kicked significant ass over the years. So a huge round of thanks to Karen Kauffman, Lesley Wachsmann, Shelli Wiggins, Jenna Cloughley, Cassie Haynes, Rachel Novak, Sue Nally, Alisha Campbell, Trisha Newman, Katherina Bohnert and more. Board members who believed in me and lifted me up were instrumental to our successes, folks like Amanda Hull, Molly Stenzel, Jessica Carpenter, Sherman Neal III, Ellen Zientek, Amy Spears, Anna Krajcik, Colleen Bell, and others.

To our photographers like Paul Robertson, I owe you a cat book! You've made roller derby look so amazing, along with Jim Dier, Danforth Johnson, Ryan Quick, Tyler Shaw, David Difuntorum, and so many others I got to know over the years. And here's to Percy, the best roller derby cat in all of history. Thank you!

For those in derby who are gone but not forgotten, you are forever tattooed on my heart. Andrea Tessler (a.k.a. Robin Drugstores), Dave Foley, Kelly Jurek, Amara Ludwig, photographer David Sacks, and the utterly unforgettable Paul Williams.

To everyone in the book, a huge thank you from the bottom of my heart. In no particular order: Jennifer Wilson, Amy Sherman, Joshua Thompson, Emma Span, Jane McManus, Todd Myers, Juliana Gonzales, April Fournier, Stefanie Madison, Kim Stegeman, Nili Goldfarb, Jeremy Stomberg, Cassie Haynes, and more. And to Laura Biagi, my OG writing nanny, thank you!

My deepest thanks to my closest friends and family who have not stopped listening to me talk about this book for two and a half years! Kris, Jack, and Patty Pennella, Karol and Bob

Foster—here it is, finally. Besties Laura Kowalzcyk, Stefanie Madison, Ryan Mount, thank you for the memes and the coffee. Juliana Gonzales, you're still the best boss I've ever had who turned into a bestie. Aedan and Trucker (a.k.a. Catman), thank you for the dog walking and polite nodding while I talked about scenes and chapters. Bob Vanstone and Kara Johnson, thank you for being generous co-parents. And, to Allora Campbell, my Bitches with Pitches, my Agent Siblings, and my dear Wallson Glass poets, thank you for always nodding along with my wild ideas! And to Sean Burns, whose critique is always a blessing.

And a massive thanks to artists Charlie Layton, Sandra Frame, photographer Paul Robertson, and all of our credited photographers for their incredible work making this book and sport look so amazing.

Finally, an eternal thanks to Miss Gusky, Mrs. Blake, Mr. Taylor, and all of my English teachers who pushed me to write my best, even when I didn't feel like it. This is only the beginning.

WORKS CITED

1.   *Rollergirls.* TV series. Aired 2006. IMDb. https://www.imdb.com/title/tt0497306/

2.   About TXRD - TXRD. "TXRD." Last modified 2024, July 10. https://txrd.com/about/

3.   RollerJam. "The Movie Database." Accessed May 18, 2025. https://www.themoviedb.org/tv/9940-rollerjam?language=en-US

4.   "The Dude of Roller Derby and His Vision (Published 2008)." The New York Times, 17 Dec. 2008, https://www.nytimes.com/2008/12/18/sports/othersports/18devildan.html.

5.   "The Dude of Roller Derby and His Vision (Published 2008)." The New York Times, 17 Dec. 2008, nttps://www.nytimes.com/2008/12/18/sports/othersports/18devildan.html.

6.   "Tough Girls Roll in the Bronx (Published 2005)." The New York Times, 15 May 2005, .

7.   Fagundes, D. (2012). Talk Derby to me: Intellectual property norms governing roller derby pseudonyms. In Texas Law Review, Texas Law Review (Vol. 90, pp. 1093–1149). https://texaslawreview.org/wp-content/uploads/2015/08/Fagundes-90-TLR-1093.pdf

8.   *Electra Woman and Dyna Girl.* TV series. Aired 1976. IMDb. https://www.imdb.com/title/tt0497306/

9.   Derby Roll Call - Derby name registration. (n.d.). https://www.derbyrollcall.com/

10.   "ESPN Slowly Introducing Online Brand for Women (Published 2010)." The New York Times, 15 Oct. 2010, .

11.   Women's Flat Track Derby Association. (2007). WFTDA STANDARDIZED FLAT TRACK ROLLER DERBY

RULES [Report]. https://static.wftda.com/rules/archive/wftda-rules-2.1.1.pdf

12. Feminism on the flat track. (2018, June 22). National Women's History Museum.

13. The Inside Press, Inc. (2011, June 6). Meet a Chappaqua roller derby mom! The Inside Press.

14. Furman, A. "Pregnancy and sports a challenging combination for female professional athletes | AP News. AP News." Last modified 2023, May 29. https://apnews.com/article/female-athletes-pregnancy-hammon-hamby-wnba-62ce78e7d3e1b547c885ae341d229027

15. "Learn More about What It's like to Be a Roller Derby Mom with the London Rollergirls, Then Watch Them Play in Malmö Tomorrow Morning at 10am CET on Wftda.Tv! | By WFTDAFacebook." By WFTDAFacebook, https://www.facebook.com/wftda/videos/learn-more-about-what-its-like-to-be-a-roller-derby-mom-with-the-london rollergi/10155722038889111/. Accessed 27 Aug. 2024.

16. "Funding DNN in 2010: Open Letter." Derby News Network, 26 July 2010, https://web.archive.org/web/20140329093349/http://www.derbynewsnetwork.com/2010/04/funding_dnn_2010_open_letter#comment-11691.

17. We did our best. | Derby News Network. (2014, September 9). https://web.archive.org/web/20160731054618/http://www.derbynews.net/2014/09/09/we-did-our-best/

18. Wiki, C. T. R. D. "Women's Flat Track Derby Association. Roller Derby Wiki." Accessed May 18, 2025. https://rollerderby.fandom.com/wiki/Women%27s_Flat_Track_Derby_Association

19. Pay Per View: The Enemy of Success." Derby News Network, 20 Sept. 2012, https://web.archive.org/web/20121108140837/http://www.derbynewsnetwork.com:80/2012/09/pay_view_enemy_success.

20. Editor & Editor. "ESPN360.com officially becomes ESPN3.com on Sunday, April 4. ESPN Press Room U.S." Last modified 2010, April 2. https://espnpressroom.com/us/press-releases/2010/04/espn360-com-officially-becomes-espn3-com-on-sunday-april

21. Derby Girl. "Goodreads." Accessed May 18, 2025. https://www.goodreads.com/book/show/1112520.Derby_Girl

22. Whip It (2009) | Drama, Sport. "IMDb." Last modified 2009, October 2. https://www.imdb.com/title/tt1172233/

23. Roller Derby Rules. (n.d.).

24. Women's Flat Track Derby Association (WFTDA), Blu, E., & Sherman, A. (2018). WFTDA-Regulation Roller Derby Track Layout Guide. In Women's Flat Track Derby Association (WFTDA). https://static.wftda.com/resources/wftda-regulation-track-layout-guide.pdf

25. Schmitt, Olivia. "ROLLER DERBY: Some People Call It One of the Fastest Growing Sports in the World." KWWL, July 2019, https://www.kwwl.com/news/cedar-rapids/roller-derby-some-people-call-it-one-of-the-fastest-growing-sports-in-the world/article_076dd338-65c7-570a-9c99-c57154209171.html.

26. Flint, J. ""Whip It" didn't need to get whipped at box office - Los Angeles Times. Los Angeles Times." Last modified 2019, July 16. https://www.latimes.com/archives/blogs/company-town-blog/story/2009-10-26/whip-it-didnt-need-to-get-whipped-a

27. Women's Flat Track Derby Association (WFTDA). (2010). WFTDA STANDARDIZED FLAT TRACK ROLLER DERBY RULES.

28. Ketchum, K. H. (2012b, May 11). WFTDA.TV on track to power women's roller derby into mainstream. Sports Video Group.

29. [ANNOUNCE] NewTek NAB 2005 press Releases - Video Group. (2005, April 18). Vizrt Forums.

30. Ketchum, K. H. (2012, May 11). WFTDA.TV on track to power women's roller derby into mainstream. Sports Video Group.

31. Philly Roller Girls. (2011). Philly Roller Girls response to WFTDA gender policy. http://www.rollerderbyinsidetrack.com/wp-content/uploads/2011/05/PRGGenderPolicy.pdf

32. WorldSkate - Skateboarding & Roller Sports - about FIRS. (n.d.). https://www.worldskate.org/news/19-about-firs/2881-about-firs.html

33. Venegas, N. "Rules for transgender Olympic athletes explained. Newsweek." Last modified 2024, July 3. https://www.newsweek.com/rules-transgender-olympic-athletes-explained-1920847#:~:text=For%20the%20Paris%2

34. Gaul, C. (April 7, 2017) Title IX and Transgender Athletes. American University Business Law Review Online. Retrieved July 10, 2018 from

35. McManus, J. "Let Suzy Hotrod take you for a ride - ESPN. ESPN.com." Last modified 2011, October 7. https://www.espn.com/

espnw/athletes-life/story/_/id/7071275/let-suzy-hotrod-take-ride

36. SUZY HOTROD - Bodies We Want 2011. (n.d.). ESPN.

37. SUZY HOTROD - Bodies We Want 2011. (n.d.-b). ESPN.

38. Tank's Tirades 1.9: Pay Per View vs. Free Per View | Roller Derby Inside Track. (n.d.).

39. Pointstreak Sports Technologies. (n.d.). Pointstreak Sports Technologies.

40. Rodriguez, S. (2014, November 4). The end of the beginning. RollerDerbyNotes.com.

41. David, S. O. "Why "27 in 5" matters - Scar of David - medium. Medium." Last modified 2018, June 15. https://medium.com/@ScarOfDavid/why-27-in-5-matters-1f11896195ce

42. Women's Flat Track Derby Association (WFTDA). (2013b). WFTDA Minimum Skills (pp. 1–4). https://static.wftda.com/resources/wftda-minimum-skills-requirements.pdf

43. Sparks, B. (2014, January 6). Oly Rollers stir up derby world with trio of transfers. Oly Sports.

44. Harris, Hope. "Nonbinary History and Definition." Point Foundation, 1 July 2022, https://pointfoundation.org/community/blog/resources/nonbinary-definition-history.

45. MRDA. (2011b, June 2). Men's Roller Derby Association releases unisex version of WFTDA Ruleset – Mens Roller Derby Association. Mens Roller Derby Association -.

46. Spencer, S., & Spencer, S. (2023, April 10). Sidelines: See Jane roll. ESPN Front Row.

47. "Why You Need To Watch The Women's Flat Track Roller Derby Championships This Weekend." Bustle, 6 Nov. 2015, https://www.bustle.com/articles/121836-why-you-need-to-watch-the-womens-flat-track-roller-derby-championships-this-weekend.

48. WFTDA. "WFTDA broadens protections for athlete gender identity. WFTDA." Last modified 2024, March 12. https://wftda.com/wftda-broadens-protections-for-athlete-gender-identity/

49. McManus, Jane. "Transgender Athletes Find Community, Support in Roller Derby." ESPN.Com, 12 Nov. 2015, https://www.espn.com/espnw/athletes-life/article/14110104/transgender-athletes-find-community-support-roller-der by.

50. Brinded, L., & Ibekwe, D. (2017, March 27). Roller derby is one of the fastest growing sports in the world — here's how it works. Business Insider.

51. Women's Flat Track Derby Association. (2024b, July 12). WFTDA membership Information » WFTDA Roller Derby Resources. WFTDA Roller Derby Resources. https://resources.wftda.org/membership/wftda-membership-information/#:~:text=51%25%20owned%20by%20leag ue%20members,of%20Flat%20Track%20Roller%20Derby.

52. X.com. (n.d.). X (Formerly Twitter).

53. Kenneally, T. "Cleveland Indians to drop Chief Wahoo logo next year. TheWrap." Last modified 2018, January 29. https://www.thewrap.com/cleveland-indians-to-drop-chief-wahoo-logo-next-year/

54. Washington Commanders | NFL Football Operations. (n.d.).

55. WFTDA. (2018, August 8). An open letter to ESPN (and to some extent, KFC) from Erica Vanstone and the WFTDA. WFTDA.

56. Holmes, Baxter. "Everything That Happened in the NBA Bubble." ESPN.Com, 8 Oct. 2020, .

57. Firger, Eric. "What the CDC's 'Substantial' and 'High' Levels of Covid-19 Transmission Actually Mean | CNN." CNN, 28 July 2021, .

58. Women's Flat Track Derby Association. (2024a, April 4). Return to Roller Derby Documents and Infection Guides » WFTDA Roller Derby Resources. WFTDA Roller Derby Resources. https://resources.wftda.org/competition/safety/return-to-roller-derby-documents-and-infection-guides/

59. Aschwanden, C. (2020, July 2). Women's roller Derby has a plan for Covid, and it kicks ass. WIRED.

Banana Pitch Press